BRINGING WOMEN IN

BRINGING WOMEN IN

Women's Issues in International Development Programs

Nüket Kardam

Lynne Rienner Publishers   Boulder & London

Published in the United States of America in 1991 by
Lynne Rienner Publishers, Inc.
1800 30th Street, Boulder, Colorado 80301

and in the United Kingdom by
Lynne Rienner Publishers, Inc.
3 Henrietta Street, Covent Garden, London WC2E 8LU

Library of Congress Cataloging-in-Publication Data
Kardam, Nüket
    Bringing women in : women's issues in international development
programs / by Nüket Kardam.
    Includes bibliographical references and index.
    ISBN 1-55587-205-0
    1. Women in development. 2. United Nations Development Programme.
3. World Bank. 4. Ford Foundation. I. Title.
HQ1240.K371990
307.1'4—dc20   90-8897
                                                                    CIP

British Cataloguing in Publication Data
A Cataloguing in Publication record for this book
is available from the British Library.

Printed and bound in the United States of America

The paper used in this publication meets the requirements
of the American National Standard for Permanence of
Paper for Printed Library Materials Z39.48-1984.

Contents

Tables and Figures

Tables

Figure

Acknowledgments

I am indebted to a number of people who helped and encouraged me to formulate, reformulate, and clarify my ideas. They include George Axinn, Michael Bratton, Donald Crone, Rita Gallin, Jack Knott, and Kathleen Staudt. I also appreciate the stimulation provided by the Office of Women in International Development and the Center for the Study of International Development at Michigan State University, whose staff, resources, and many seminars gave me the opportunity to delve into the issues of women and development assistance. I am grateful to the Thoman Foundation for a fellowship that enabled me to travel to Washington, D.C., and New York to conduct interviews and collect documents. Without the help of the staff members in the World Bank, the United Nations Development Programme, and the Ford Foundation, who must remain anonymous, and who gave me their time, insights, and friendship, my research could not have been done. I would also like to thank the staff of Lynne Rienner Publishers for their support and Pamela Ferdinand for her editorial assistance.

My husband and colleague, Donald Crone, deserves a special acknowledgment for his significant academic involvement at every stage of the project, as well as for taking over the lion's share of family responsibilities while I disappeared for countless hours into my office. I thank my mother, Leman Kardam, my daughter, Maya, and my son, Timur, for being so thoroughly part of my life and so understanding of an absent-minded, preoccupied family member. I have come to understand that without a supportive, loving family that reminds one of the joys of everyday life, it is virtually impossible to finish a long-term project that requires tremendous commitment, patience, and persistence. The sole responsibility for the final product, of course, rests with me.

Nüket Kardam

Introduction

International social movements have important implications for governments and for the organizations that generally play the leading role in setting international norms. The women's movement, along with the environmental movement, is engaged in changing the way development issues are defined. The questions of how the discourse on development changes over time and who plays a role in the debate are significant for all those involved in both theoretical and practical aspects of development. How this discourse infiltrates and affects concrete programs and projects is another puzzling issue that has important implications for the design and delivery of development assistance. This book highlights some aspects of these significant questions.

In the 1970s, an international social movement emerged that had as one of its objectives the altering of the development assistance regime toward the formulation and implementation of more gender-sensitive policies.[1] As norms and rules began to change to include women in development assistance, how did various development agencies respond?

Many studies have examined how regimes form, work, and decline,[2] but few trace how regimes affect policy formulation and implementation within specific international organizations. Regime analysis tends to remain at an abstract level, with little attention to ways in which specific organizational contexts may affect the translation of expectations into action. This book combines the insights of both regime and organization theory to analyze how the international women's movement has attempted to alter the norms of the development assistance regime, and how three development agencies have responded.

The adverse impact of agency policies on poor women of developing countries has been documented since the beginning of the 1970s. The problems affecting policymaking were identified as (1) ingrained attitudes, values, and perceptions among development personnel that did not correspond to reality; (2) a lack of information and data on women; and (3) a shortfall in resources allocated to women. To remedy this situation, three major policy recommendations were made: (1) resocialization of personnel through training and education programs; (2) redirection of research and data collection to include women; and (3) allocation of resources to employ more female development professionals to set up and monitor programs related to women in development.[3] The explanation for the slow implementation of these proposals has too often been circular, with attention simply redirected to the original problems.

We need to ask some questions: How do social movements that enter the political arena and attempt to redefine issues (or even to create issues) influence existing norms, rules, and regulations—the existing regimes? What are the determinants of success for regime formation, and what chance do international movements have to affect existing regimes?[4] And how do organizations respond to new issues? What determines their performance on a new issue?

My thesis is that the international women's movement, as a social movement, has been able to penetrate the relatively weak, decentralized development assistance regime, but is constrained by the very nature of that regime from turning general ideas into specific, clear, and implementable policies. The responses of development agencies to women in development (WID) issues are shaped by the nature of their relations with other actors of the development assistance regime and by how well those new issues fit into organizational goals and procedures. "Policy entrepreneurs" within agencies can and do act on behalf of WID issues, framing them in ways that will be consistent with organizational goals and procedures, taking advantage of their agency's position in relation to other members of the regime, and developing political clout in order to influence policymaking. Through these means, WID advocates are able to promote a meaningful response.

My conclusions are based on an examination of three development agencies—the United Nations Development Programme (UNDP), the World Bank, and the Ford Foundation—and their responses to WID issues, which I assess in terms of the extent of change made in procedures, programs, and staff. Chapter 1 lays out the theoretical basis and discusses the rise of the international women's movement. Chapters 2, 3, and 4 deal with the UNDP, World Bank, and Ford Foundation and describe the extent of change and explain it in light of regime and organizational characteristics. The concluding chapter summarizes the central themes of the argument and discusses the findings that emerge from the analysis.

The empirical materials for this book were collected at the headquarters of the three agencies during spring and summer 1986, spring 1988, and fall 1989. I interviewed fifty staff members in the World Bank, thirty in the UNDP, and fifteen in the Ford Foundation. Although I sought a stratified sample that covered the staff and management in each office, the samples are not representative in the statistical sense; they are "snowball samples" in the sense that I was given names of other people to interview as I conducted my research. The number of women in each sample is higher than women's proportional representation in each agency, a disproportionality caused by their special interest in gender issues as they relate to development planning. My discussion also draws on documents made available to me by these agencies.

It is important to be clear about what this book does not do. The three agencies discussed here are not meant to be a representative sample of all actors within the development assistance regime; rather, they are presented as case studies, meant to provide a closer look at WID-related activities in order to illustrate how advocacy and response interrelate. I chose them to represent three major categories with different organizational characteristics: a multilateral aid agency, a multilateral development bank, and a nongovernmental charitable organization. The agencies differ enough to permit showing how variance in performance in the same policy area may be related to different organizational characteristics.

Notes

1. I define international development assistance agencies as all those that work in developing countries in the field of development assistance, regardless of whether they are bilateral, multilateral, or nongovernmental organizations.

2. See, e.g., Stephen D. Krasner, ed., *International Regimes* (Ithaca, NY: Cornell University Press, 1983).

3. See, e.g., Adrienne Germain, "Poor Rural Women: A Policy Perspective," *Journal of International Affairs* 30, 2 (1976–77): 161–172; Barbara Rogers, *The Domestication of Women: Discrimination in Developing Societies* (London: Tavistock, 1980); and Kathleen Staudt, "Bureaucratic Resistance to Women's Programs: The Case of Women in Development," in *Women, Power and Policy*, ed. Ellen Bonaparth (New York: Pergamon Press, 1982).

4. See Oran Young, "The Politics of International Regime Formation: Managing Natural Resources and the Environment," *International Organization* 43, 3 (Summer 1989): 349–375.

1

Women in Development: Adaptability of International Development Assistance Agencies

Explanations of Policy Change

The adaptability of international organizations and their response to new issues are important to both development theorists and practitioners, but the nature of the debate on these phenomena has differed depending on one's theoretical perspective. International agencies have traditionally been treated as creatures of nation-states, regarded as having little independent influence over their own operations. The viewpoint owes a good deal to the realist perspective in international relations, which focuses on external factors to explain the policies of international organizations, because it assumes that states and their interests determine policy outcomes. More recently, with the increasing emphasis on international regimes—the norms, rules, and decisionmaking processes at the international level—the study of international organizations has virtually disappeared in favor of studying "trade regimes," "monetary regimes," or "ocean regimes," for example.[1] Study of international organizations has further suffered from lack of attention to the insights of organization theory in such matters as how, for example, organizational goals and procedures influence performance.[2]

The realist and the regime analyses offer limited explanatory power for understanding change in international agencies. It is now apparent that member states' voting power and preferences do not automatically decide policy outcomes in specific international organizations. And although international regimes are significant, different organizations may perform differently within the same regime; some agencies may play a leading role in changing regime norms, others may be passive. It is necessary to go inside international agencies in order to understand organizational constraints and opportunities for change.

Policy change can be explained in terms of structure and choice factors. Structure refers to the nature and characteristics of the regime within which international agencies function and to organizational goals and procedures. Although structural constraints can significantly affect policy outcomes, they cannot totally determine them. Choice factors play a role also. Individual actors can still exercise choice by deciding, for example, what kind of bargaining strategies to use to effect change. But these actors do not choose the circumstances in which they make decisions; rather, they intervene within a particular context. Thus, policy outcomes are best seen as the result of an interaction between individual choice and structural conditions.[3]

Structural Factors

The norms, rules, and regulations of the development assistance regime affect policy outcomes within agencies, and changes in those norms and rules can be expected to influence all the actors within the regime. That being the case, influencing regime actors by including women's issues in the norms would influence policy affecting women. However, all development agencies would not be uniformly affected because the specific goals and procedures of each agency also play a role in determining policy outcomes. As organization theorists maintain, organizations influence the policy process because they are not passive but rather are live collectivities with distinct goals and procedures. These goals and procedures determine the effectiveness and efficiency of organizational activities[4] and also determine how organizations interact with their environment. This interaction can be characterized as interdependent: The organization exchanges political support, information, or financial resources with important actors in its environment in order to survive.[5]

An "organizational goal" is an ambiguous concept—many theorists have grappled with it—but it is safe to say that all organizations are created to achieve some identifiable ends, some publicly stated goals. Goals do not change, even though different executive heads may emphasize different strategies to achieve them.[6] By choosing one goal over another, organizations can also choose a particular interpretation of the environment—that is, a value system on which the chosen goal rests. This value system could also be termed *organizational ideology* and be defined as "sets of beliefs that provide explanations for phenomena, suggest appropriate actions and bind together the organization's adherents."[7] When an organization responds to a new issue, how the issue comports with the organizational goal plays an important role in determining the extent of the response.

Organizations adopt certain procedures to achieve their goals, and these also determine how an organization responds to new issues. Procedures, broadly defined, include skills, knowledge, training of employees (including the approaches and strategies used),[8] and decisionmaking techniques (such as economic analysis, technical analysis, or analysis based on social science techniques) and structure (whether decisionmaking is centralized, decentralized, or a combination). Particular procedures call for staff members with special skills, knowledge, and training. Because different professions bring different policy definitions, data, and methodologies to the policy arena,[9] fitting a new issue into the existing procedures and ensuring its acceptance by the staff that uses these procedures should increase the chances of its incorporation into agency activities.

Among studies dealing with the effects of professional conceptions of policy on outcomes, Ascher's analysis of the World Bank demonstrates that adding new criteria (e.g., equity, the role of women in development, environmental protection, human rights) to the desiderata of development has met with resistance. He offers this explanation: "Many professionals in the World Bank have been reluctant to incorporate new considerations in formulating development strategies if they require modes of analysis less rigorous than the traditional economic framework."[10] A study by Levy, Meltsner, and Wildavsky illustrates how in several policy areas in urban government, professional conceptions of policy determine the types of actions taken by city departments and the corresponding outcomes for citizens.[11]

In short, structural characteristics are very important in the explanation of response to a new issue. In the case of WID issues, the position of a development assistance agency within the regime, as well as the consistency of WID issues with the goals and procedures of that agency, may increase its extent of response. One should not, however, see the response to a new issue in deterministic terms; the outcome is the result of both structural and choice factors.

Choice Factors

Without advocates willing to bargain on its behalf, a new issue will not automatically be incorporated into an agency's activities.[12] The structural conditions may set the stage within which individual actors bargain over implementation,[13] but required is the conscious choice made by some staff members to act as advocates and to bring specific bargaining strategies to bear on promoting a new issue.

Polsby suggests that policy innovations are initiated by policy entrepreneurs—interest groups and persons who actively identify new issues and specialize in acquiring and deploying knowledge about them.[14] Policy advocacy can be employed formally or informally. In their formal roles, policy entrepreneurs oversee advocacy administration, a method by which theories on organizational change can be linked to

actual practice; advocacy administrators promote new, nonroutine programs.[15] Policy advocates may also form informal structures to promote
change both within and outside the organization. In organization theory,
formal structures designed to regulate behavior in the service of specific
goals are seen to be greatly affected—supplemented, eroded, transformed—by the emergence of informal structures, which are those based
on the personal characteristics or resources of the specific participants.[16]

Policy advocates need both new information and political clout to
promote a new issue. Polsby suggests that in order to bring a policy into
being, the policy entrepreneurs skillfully mobilize facts that can justify
action and identify and cultivate allies. In other words, policymaking is
both a technical undertaking and a political process, and actual policies
are made through a combination of facts and power. Wilson has pointed
out that innovation requires influence because it requires getting people
to accept new ideas.[17] Wildavsky goes further: Unless building support
for policies is an integral part of designing them, their proponents are
setting themselves up for disappointment.[18]

The move toward integration of WID issues into the development
assistance regime and the consistency of WID issues with organizational
goals and procedures do not, on their own, guarantee attention to WID
issues. Without the efforts of WID policy entrepreneurs, the incentive to
respond may remain negligible; the more bargaining power WID advocates have, the more extensive the response is likely to be. Before I present the case studies, I discuss the rise of the international women's
movement in the 1970s and its efforts to integrate women's issues into
the development assistance regime. These changes at the international
level have encouraged all development agencies to pay attention to
women in their activities.

WID Issues and the Development Assistance Regime

Oran Young suggests that the emergence of effective leadership is one of
the conditions of successful regime formation.[19] Social movements, such
as the international women's movement, have generally not been considered important leaders in regime formation, nor has the effect of social
movements in policymaking been adequately explored.[20] However, social
movements can act as effective catalysts in changing regimes, and the
women's movement has assumed leadership in altering the norms, rules,
and regulations of the international development assistance regime so
that they take women into account.

Social movements are a primary means of socializing conflict, of taking private disputes and making them political ones.[21] A social move-

ment aims to enter the political arena and expand "the scope of conflict."[22] McWilliams argues that issues previously nonpolitical will almost inevitably become political whenever two conditions apply: (1) "when reality comes to be perceptibly discordant with social myths"; and (2) "when there is the opportunity to compare notes on personal unhappiness."[23] Freeman, in building on the second point, proposes three criteria regarding the origins of social movements: (1) a preexisting communications network; (2) perceptivity of this network to the new ideas of the incipient movement; and (3) a crisis that galvanizes the network into spontaneous action in a new direction or the existence of skillful organizers.[24] The international women's movement, according to these criteria, is a social movement—that is, it is not one single or national pressure group but many groups. And although the movement centered itself in the United Nations Decade for Women conferences in the 1970s and 1980s, it has taken many forms, and there have been many different stimuli to indigenous activity all around the world.[25]

The term "women in development" was coined by the women's committee of the Washington, D.C., chapter of the Society for International Development.[26] This group moved to influence the policy of the US Agency for International Development (USAID) by testifying at the congressional hearings that frame US foreign assistance policies. From this group came the concepts that underlie the Percy amendment to the 1973 "New Directions" legislation. New Directions constituted a series of amendments to the 1972 Foreign Assistance act and required focusing assistance programs on food, nutrition, health and population, education, and human resources. The Percy amendment, sponsored by Senator Charles Percy, stipulated that bilateral and multilateral assistance programs be administered so as to give particular attention to those programs, projects, and activities that tend to integrate women into the national economies of foreign countries and mandated the USAID to implement the guidelines.[27]

What factors made the passage of this amendment possible?[28] First, there were strong and influential women who supported it and who came from mainstream and scholarly organizations. Second, these women had the backing of the women's movement in the United States, and because that movement had acquired some political clout, Senator Charles Percy had an interest in satisfying women voters. Third, the request to integrate women into development was consistent with the values expressed in the New Directions legislation. This legislation, concerned with helping the poorer sections of Third World populations, should naturally be concerned with women, who usually constitute the poorer and less powerful sections of Third World societies. Finally, the Percy amendment did not carry any appropriations—the monies were attached to the New Directions law—thus, adding the amendment neither carried much fiscal cost nor entailed any political cost for its sponsor.

As a result of the Percy amendment, an Office of Women in Development was established in the USAID, whose field missions, offices, and bureaus were charged with integrating women (as both agents and beneficiaries) into the mainstream of the agency's programming process from concept and design through review, implementation, and final evaluation. Bureaus and field missions were also asked to encourage international development agencies and other donors and private, voluntary organizations to give specific attention to the role of women in development.

Beginning in 1970, WID activities within the UN system also increased substantially. Members of the United Nations, its specialized agencies, and all organs and agencies within the system were invited to cooperate in achieving WID objectives and targets and to make available adequate staff and resources for the advancement of women. The 1970 resolution of the General Assembly on International Action for the Advancement of Women led to the organization of an Interregional Meeting of Experts on the Role of Women in Economic and Social Development by the UN Division of Social Development in June 1972; in 1974, an International Forum on the Role of Women in Population and Development was held as part of the activities of the World Population Year. In 1975, the World Conference of the International Women's Year was held in Mexico, and the period 1975–1985 was declared the UN Decade for Women. The Mexico conference was followed by a mid-Decade conference in Copenhagen in 1980 and an end-Decade conference in Nairobi in 1985. Many observers have noted that the impetus to include women's issues in UN conferences came from the informal WID network, particularly from supporters in nongovernmental development agencies.[29] This network is reported to have organized "countermeetings" because women and women's issues had been continually excluded from UN conference agendas.[30] Boulding noted that "most of the women, no matter how much knowledge they had, stood aside at these conferences as petitioners and protesters."[31]

By the close of the Nairobi conference, there was no question of the consolidation of an international women's movement on a global basis. In fact, overlapping the official intergovernmental conference in Nairobi, nongovernmental organizations (NGOs) sponsored Forum 85, which drew fourteen thousand people. Represented were organizations from all over the world: Development Alternatives with Women in a New Era; Women's Studies International; General Federation of Jordanian Women; National Nurses Association of Kenya; Third World Movement

Against the Exploitation of Women; Housewives in Dialogue; and Seven Sisters College Delegation, USA. Participants attended over fifteen hundred workshops and seminars on a wide variety of subjects of concern to women.

The outcome of the Nairobi conference was the publication of a document[32] that formulated guidelines for implementation, by national governments and international agencies, of strategies for specific sectors, such as employment, health, education, food, water, agriculture, industry, housing, and the environment. These strategies stipulated that bilateral and multilateral agencies' policies for WID assistance should involve all parts of donor organizations, and that programs and policies for women in development should be incorporated into all applicable aid and agency procedures relating to sectoral and project levels.[33] Thus, rules and norms were established, and efforts were made to set up compliance mechanisms whereby UN development agencies, at least, could be held responsible for the implementation of WID policy. These efforts were facilitated by the leadership of bilateral development agencies of Canada, the Netherlands, Sweden, and Norway.

Exogenous shocks or crises, according to Young, increase the probability of success in negotiating the terms of international regimes.[34] The international women's movement formed around a crisis situation in the 1970s: increased poverty in developing countries and uncertainty about the effectiveness of conventional development strategies. An informal network of female professionals and researchers in the development field documented both how women's situation in the Third World had actually worsened as a result of development and that the reality of their situation failed to match the descriptions and definitions propagated by development planners and practitioners. The existing women's networks adopted these new issues and attempted through the forums of the UN conferences to convince governments and international development agencies that women and men are affected differently by development policies and that those policies need consciously to take the special needs and capabilities of women into account.

Studies documented that women's status often declined because development planners treated women mainly in their reproductive roles, failing to consider women's productivity or to provide them with resources such as access to credit and new technology, even in activities traditionally performed by women. These planners followed an earlier pattern: Colonial administrators, contributing their own definitions of appropriate roles for women, had begun the process of female marginalization by training men only and by structuring access to credit and other resources to the male as "head of household."[35] Ester Boserup's path-breaking *Women's Role in Economic Development*, published in 1970, argued that improved technology in farming actually lowered women's status by reducing their access to productive work. She found other aspects of modernization also proving detrimental to women: Urbanization cuts women off from their kinship support networks, there are fewer jobs in the modern sector, and what jobs are available are often closed to women because of sex stereotyping. Urban women throughout the world are the main participants in the so-called informal sector, which is primarily petty trading and, often, prostitution.

Women are not recognized as a development problem because it is assumed they will be cared for by male heads of household and that their marginalization from economic activities is both inevitable and appropriate; arguments that favor directing resources to women are denied on the grounds that women are "less productive" or "too traditional." Development assistance may be directed toward women, but only in their status as mothers (nutrition and maternal and child health programs), potential mothers (population programs), or auxiliary workers (handicrafts programs). Women are seen as reproducers, not producers; welfare cases, not workers.[36]

These criticisms were formulated from a liberal feminist viewpoint that supported equality of opportunity for women and advocated "increased political and economic participation for women." Efficiency and equity justified attention to WID issues. It was argued that discrimination is not economically rational; if women are marginal to economic development programs, it is at the cost of greater productivity. Ignoring women also hinders equitable development because any strategy that disproportionately favors men cannot be considered an equitable approach.[37] The main objective of a WID policy is defined by Staudt:

> The essence of a Women in Development approach is to ascertain what women actually want and do within a society and provide them with opportunities and skills and resources to enhance that participation. . . . [T]he WID strategy rests on creating more rational and evenhanded planning which takes into account the sex division of labor, fair returns for labor, and the equitable infusion of new opportunities and resources to all members of a given community.[38]

The discourse about women and development emphasized the contribution women would make to the attainment of general development goals. In other words, the discourse was defined in terms of "the common good"—the terms were contractual rather than confrontational. As Young indicates:

> Institutional bargaining can succeed only when the issues at stake lend themselves to contractarian interactions. Those engaged in efforts to

form international regimes experience incentives to approach this process as a problem-solving exercise aimed at reaching agreement on the terms of a social contract when the absence of a fully specified zone of agreement encourages integrative bargaining and the presence of imperfect information ensures that a veil of uncertainty prevails.[39]

Regime formation requires finding ways to institutionalize cooperation and collective action, which means promoting reformist rather than radical policies as well as problem-solving rather than confrontational approaches. In order to build a new regime, then, the international women's movement has defined and advocated changes within the confines of given institutions. As Jaquette observed: "While U.N. women's conferences, and their mix of liberal and socialist feminists, New International Order advocates, and others spend considerable time identifying and debating the source of women's subordination, from male prejudice to international capitalism, their solutions are limited to practical, incremental bureaucratic reform and women's pressure activity."[40] Staudt suggests some explanations for this moderate tack; she argues that contemporary feminism makes no great demands but instead presses for issues within the confines of given institutions:

The explanation for this reticence is obvious to those working with existing bureaucracies, states and international institutions. The resistance to a redistribution of social values and resources along gender egalitarian lines and a redefinition of politics itself is profound, and politically weak women's groups are easy to ignore or dismiss. Consequently, active women articulate narrow goals, using grounds for which the institutions will be receptive. This results in building on existing conceptions of men and women, and using arguments which advance the interests of institutions, which may or may not conflict with those of women. The politics of contemporary feminism is implicitly a politics of pluralism, and its goals of more egalitarian policies are reformist, pluralist, and incremental, through separate women's interest groups.[41]

The general goal of the international women's movement is to empower women, and the movement solicits the help of governments and aid bureaucracies in this process. The movement has succeeded in putting women's issues on the agenda of donor agencies, but not without compromising. Empowering women implies fundamental changes in gender relations as well as in political, economic, and social structures that relegate women to a less powerful position. However, the solutions proposed have emphasized integrating women into development activities based on practical, incremental, bureaucratic reforms and women's pressure group activities. The reasons for this outcome relate not only to the necessity to be engaged in contractual interactions but also to the nature of social movements. Once a social movement enters the political realm, it is usually constrained by the limitations of this realm. There already exist many concrete, accepted "rules of the game" that newcomers are expected to abide by.[42] Thus, social movements have to frame their demands within existing definitions and within existing institutions. These institutions, of course, by their ability to reward or punish efforts for change with success or defeat, often can reshape a social movement, leading it to conform to the norms of behavior the better to participate in the institutions but often to forsake its major goals.

How did efforts to include WID issues within the development assistance regime affect the performance of specific international agencies? There is little evidence that actors' expectations have converged or that there is any across-the-board acceptance or implementation of WID policies by all relevant actors. There are, however, varying degrees of acceptance by international development agencies, as well as by governments, of the importance of WID issues in development. Regime changes at the international level are bound to remain abstract and vague unless further research can demonstrate how they shape concrete policy changes in the relevant institutions and how those institutions respond to and mold that regime in different ways.

Notes

1. Krasner, *International Regimes.*
2. See, e.g., David A. Kay and Harold K. Jacobson, *Environmental Protection: The International Dimension* (Totowa, NJ: Allanheld & Osmun, 1983); Judith Tendler, *Inside Foreign Aid* (Baltimore, MD: Johns Hopkins University Press, 1975); and William Ascher, "New Development Approaches and the Adaptability of International Agencies: The Case of the World Bank," *International Organization* 37, 3 (Summer 1983): 415–439, for examples of studies that emphasize organizational variables.
3. I am indebted to Michael Bratton for this particular conception of policy change.
4. Gayle Ness and Steven Brechin, "Bridging the Gap: International Organizations as Organizations," *International Organization* 42, 2 (Spring 1988): 245–273.
5. Richard Scott, *Organizations: Rational, Natural and Open Systems* (Englewood Cliffs, NJ: Prentice-Hall, 1987).
6. Robert Cox, "The Executive Head: An Essay in Leadership in International Organization," in *International Organization: Politics and Process,* eds. Leland Goodrich and David Kay (Madison: University of Wisconsin Press, 1973).

7. Robert Cox and Harold Jacobson, *The Anatomy of Influence* (New Haven, CT: Yale University Press, 1974), p. 22.

8. Scott, *Organizations*.

9. Jack Knott, "The Multiple and Ambiguous Roles of Professionals in Public Policymaking," *Knowledge Creation, Diffusion, Utilization* 8, 1 (1986): 131–153.

10. Ascher, "New Development Approaches," p. 428.

11. Frank Levy, Arthur Meltsner, and Aaron Wildavsky, *Urban Outcomes* (Berkeley: University of California Press, 1974), cited in Knott, "Multiple and Ambiguous Roles."

12. This is also Karin Himmelstrand's argument in "Can an Aid Bureaucracy Empower Women? The Case of SIDA," *Issue: A Journal of Opinion* 37, 2 (1989): 37–43.

13. Eugene Bardach, *The Implementation Game* (Cambridge: Massachusetts Institute of Technology Press, 1978).

14. Nelson Polsby, *Policy Innovation in the United States* (New Haven, CT: Yale University Press, 1984).

15. Anthony Downs, *Inside Bureaucracy* (Boston: Little, Brown, 1966).

16. Scott, *Organizations*.

17. James Q. Wilson, "Innovation in Organization: Notes Toward a Theory," in *Approaches to Organizational Design*, ed. J. D. Thompson (Pittsburgh, PA: University of Pittsburgh Press, 1966).

18. Aaron Wildavsky, "The Self-Evaluating Organization," *Public Administration Review* (September-October 1972): 517.

19. Young, "Politics of International Regime Formation."

20. Jo Freeman has explored such effects. She traces the evolution of the women's liberation movement and its policy impact; *The Politics of Women's Liberation* (New York: Longman, 1975).

21. Ibid.

22. E.E. Schattschneider, *The Semi-Sovereign People* (New York: Holt, Rinehart & Winston, 1960).

23. Nancy McWilliams, "Contemporary Feminism, Consciousness-Raising, and Changing Views of the Political," in *Women and Politics*, ed. Jane Jaquette (New York: Wiley, 1974), p. 160.

24. Freeman, *Politics of Women's Liberation*, pp. 48-50.

25. See, e.g., Irene Tinker, ed., *Women in Washington: Advocates for Public Policy* (New York: Pergamon Press; London: Sage, 1983); Georgina Ashworth, "The United Nations Women's Conference and International Linkages with the Women's Movement," in *Pressure Groups in the Global System*, ed. E. Willets (London: Francis Pinter, 1982).

26. Irene Tinker, "Women in Development," in Tinker, *Women in Washington*.

27. U.S. Department of State, Agency for International Development, "Integration of Women into National Economies," Policy Determination 60, 16 September 1974.

28. These factors are cited in Tinker, "Women in Development."

29. Patricia Maguire, *Women in Development: An Alternative Analysis*

(Amherst: Center for International Education, University of Massachusetts, 1984).

30. Elise Boulding, *Women: The Fifth World* (New York: Foreign Policy Association, 1980).

31. Ibid.

32. UN, *Nairobi Forward-Looking Strategies for the Advancement of Women* (New York: UN Division for Economic and Social Information, April 1986).

33. Ibid., pp. 78–80.

34. Young, "Politics of International Regime Formation."

35. Jane Jaquette, "Women and Modernization Theory: A Decade of Feminist Criticism," *World Politics* 34, 2 (1982): 267–284.

36. See, e.g., Ester Boserup, *Women's Role in Economic Development* (New York: St. Martin's Press, 1970); Irene Tinker and M. B. Bramsen, eds., *Women and World Development* (Washington, DC: Overseas Development Council, 1976); Barbara Lewis, *Invisible Farmers: Women and the Crisis in Agriculture* (Washington, DC: USAID, 1981); and Mayra Buvinic et al., *Women's Issues in Third World Poverty* (Baltimore, MD: Johns Hopkins University Press, 1983).

37. Kathleen Staudt, *Women, Foreign Assistance and Advocacy Administration* (New York: Praeger, 1985), p. 43.

38. Staudt, "Bureaucratic Resistance to Women's Programs," p. 265.

39. Young, "Politics of International Regime Formation," pp. 366–367.

40. Jane Jaquette, "Copenhagen, 1980: Women in Development, Feminism and the New International Economic Order," paper presented at the annual meeting of the American Sociological Association, Toronto, Canada, 25–29 August 1981, pp. 8ff, cited in Kathleen Staudt, "Women's Politics and Capitalist Transformation in Sub-Saharan Africa," Women in Development Working Paper Series No. 54 (East Lansing: Michigan State University 1984).

41. Staudt, "Women's Politics and Capitalist Transformation," p. 17.

42. Freeman, *Politics of Women's Liberation*, p. 5.

2

The Tripartite System
of the United Nations
Development Programme

The UNDP was created in 1966 to coordinate and administer UN resources for technical cooperation within a trilateral system made up of the UNDP, specialized UN agencies contracted by the UNDP to execute projects, and recipient governments. The UNDP was born out of the convergence of two organizations, the Expanded Programme of Technical Assistance for Economic Development of Underdeveloped Countries (EPTA), founded in 1950, and the United Nations Special Fund, founded in 1959.

The EPTA was set up as a result of a call for technical assistance by the General Assembly of the United Nations in 1948. Citing the lack of expert personnel and technical organization in underdeveloped areas, the General Assembly on 4 December 1948 authorized funds to enable the secretary-general to organize international teams of experts through the UN or its specialized agencies to advise governments on economic development; to assist in training experts and technicians both abroad and in the developing countries themselves; and to assist governments in obtaining technical personnel, equipment, and supplies and in organizing their development efforts, including the exchange of information on common problems.[1] The UN Special Fund, on the other hand, functioned as a capital development fund, financing extensive surveys and feasibility studies to facilitate new capital investments. A report titled "Technical Assistance for Economic Development," issued in 1949, laid out the basic guidelines for UN development activities. These guidelines, which are still operative today, reflect principles that stress the sovereignty, independence, and self-reliance of the developing countries as participants of development programs.

Structurally, the UNDP is a decentralized organization, with 116 field offices around the world and a relatively small head office in New York. Approximately 500 of the UNDP's 860 professional staff members are located in the field offices, which are managed by resident representatives (resreps). The UNDP staff rotates between field offices and the New

York headquarters, which is organized into four regional bureaus, with desk officers for countries. These regional bureaus are for Africa, the Arab states, Asia and the Pacific, and Latin America and the Caribbean. The head office also houses the Bureau for Program and Policy Evaluation, which provides policy guidance; the Division of Global and Interregional Projects, which deals with projects initiated at UNDP headquarters in response to worldwide needs identified at global conferences; the special unit for Technical Cooperation Among Developing Countries; and the Office for Project Execution, which implements a small number of projects on behalf of the UNDP, instead of contracting them out to UN specialized agencies.

Assistance from the UNDP comes on grant terms, but recipient governments must make allocations from their domestic budgets to meet such project needs as local infrastructure, salaries of national personnel, and recurrent expenditures. The UNDP's resources are allocated to countries on the basis of an internationally agreed formula, the indicative planning figure (IPF), which is the amount projected to be available for program activities in a country over a five-year period. The IPF is based on a country's population and per capita gross national product level, ensuring that the largest amounts of assistance go to the poorest and most populous countries.

The UNDP receives its funds in the form of voluntary contributions from the member governments of the UN or its affiliated agencies. Contributions pledged for the UNDP core and UNDP-administered funds totaled over US$1 billion for 1989.[2] The top contributors are the United States, Sweden, the Netherlands, Norway, and Japan.[3] The UNDP is accountable to a Governing Council with representatives from forty-eight developed and developing countries. The council functions on a one member–one vote basis. The developing countries, which are also the recipients of UNDP funds, have a dominant role because of their numerical majority.

The UNDP estimates its volume of contributions and plans its activities on the basis of five-year development cooperation cycles. Programs are drawn up jointly by the recipient national governments, the resreps, and the participating organization. These country programs seek to coincide with the country's own development plan, identifying the role and phasing of the UNDP's inputs that fall within the country's development objectives. The governments, in cooperation with the UNDP field office, present a plan of projects to be undertaken with UNDP funding, which is then appraised by the head office. The regional and global programs are funded through regional IPFs allocated by the Governing Council, drafted by UNDP regional bureaus in the headquarters, and finalized in consultation with governments concerned, UN regional commissions, and the UN specialized agencies.

Response to WID Issues

Policy and Procedures

The first UNDP guidelines on WID issues, produced in 1977, were stated in general terms and did not provide staff with any specific measures by which to implement a WID policy. The 1977 guidelines are titled "Guidelines on the Integration of Women in Development" and are included in the Policy and Program Manual, the operations manual of the UNDP.[4] It is indicated in the introduction to the guidelines that the administrator is anxious to see all projects examined from the standpoint of women's role in development. Areas wherein women should be particularly considered are identified as "education, agriculture, food production, handicrafts and health services."[5]

The first two parts of the guidelines contain a general discussion of the problem of women's role in development. Following is a typical paragraph:

> There is, of course, a price tag on the correction or reversal of the tendency to exclude women from the modernization process. All change carries a cost of some kind. In view of the nature of the problem, the process is generally one of reallocation of resources across the board—with the obvious goal of increasing the overall return on development investment in so doing. The timetable and magnitude of the reallocation will have to be considered on a case by case basis. For certain activities the basic problem may be as simple as giving women access to existing services—for training and credit, for example. Often special or complementary facilities are called for. In all instances, the solution will be facilitated by improved information about women's role in society and by women's inclusion in the public decision-making process.[6]

For specific guidelines on how to include women in the UNDP's activities, this document simply cited other sources: "More specific advice concerning the diverse problems of how to better integrate women in the development process has been given the form of an annotated list of references."[7] This section refers the reader to the guidelines of other development agencies, such as the United Nations Fund for Population Activities (UNFPA), and to the recommendations produced by UN conferences and literature on WID issues by scholars.

The vague nature of the UNDP's directions to staff is an indication that no particular procedural or programmatic changes were planned to deal with gender issues in the agency's development assistance activities. The guidelines were revised and made more specific nine years later, in

1986, at the request of the Governing Council to the new administrator, William Draper III, by Gloria Scott, the former adviser on women in development at the World Bank. The resulting "UNDP Programme Advisory Note [PAN]—Women in Development" is much more extensive. Directed at governments, the UNDP, and other organizations in the UN development system, the PAN suggests the following means by which to implement WID policy: the introduction of WID issues in donor consultations or roundtables where they can be discussed as part of the examination of development priorities of the particular country and its related needs for technical cooperation; and the consideration of WID issues at project identification and design stages, when general questions about women in the country or region, or the type of interventions being considered are raised. The PAN also provides a framework for project analysis that includes an activity profile and an access and control profile on women. Furthermore, it provides an extensive account of how women may be considered and what questions need to be addressed in the identification, design, implementation, and monitoring, and the review and evaluation stages of projects in eleven different sectors and areas: development planning; education and training; agriculture, animal husbandry, and fisheries; forestry and energy; industry; small-scale enterprises in the informal sector; population, health, and nutrition; water supply and sanitation; credit; employment; and the data base.

"Programme Implementation—Women in Development: The Implementation Strategy," a report submitted to the UNDP's Governing Council in June 1986, expands on these policy guidelines:

1. The issues of WID will be considered as part of the preparation of each country programme. The Resident Representative will make proposals on the subject in the note submitted to the Government as part of the planning procedure. These proposals, as well as proposals by the Government, will subsequently be discussed in detail as the planning of the country programme proceeds. In the final country programme proposal, the nature of women's participation in each project or area of assistance will be identified. These issues will be translated into specific work plans at the time or preparation of the project document.

2. WID issues will be monitored and reviewed in the course of implementation of country programmes and the results will be included in all implementation reports and assessments.

3. The same principles will be applied in the preparation of regional, interregional and global programmes, i.e., women's interests will be taken into account at all stages of preparation, implementation and evaluation of these programs.[8]

The Division of Women in Development, established in 1987 within the Bureau for Program and Policy Evaluation, has issued a comprehensive document that outlines how WID issues will be integrated into country programming, project cycle, monitoring, and evaluation.[9] This document encompasses previous proposals along with some new ones. At the country programming level, the suggestion is for the resrep to indicate in the UNDP's position paper how women can be included in the country program. WID issues should also be discussed in the national technical cooperation assessment and programs and in roundtables. For the project cycle, the division has proposed the use of a project review form in all projects, which includes questions on the pertinence of women's issues to the project in order to generate proposals that specify how the project will integrate women.[10] The project review form also asks for information regarding the relative numbers of women and men active in the sector in which the project is located; whether WID issues are reflected in project objectives, outputs, and activities; whether women are beneficiaries of the project; and the actual number of women and men engaged as project personnel or involved in training. The review form also invites comments, explanations, and suggestions for improved gender-responsiveness. All field offices were instructed to fill out this form for a representative sample of projects; the 1,258 forms received corresponded to approximately one-fourth of the UNDP's over five thousand projects.[11]

In 1987, two project review mechanisms began to provide for more systematic inclusion of women in development: WID issues are considered by the project appraisal committees (established in 1986) in all regional bureaus as well as by the action committee, which is chaired by the administrator and composed of senior management officials. This committee, which provides input into all projects costing over $700,000, includes the director of the Division for Women in Development, providing her with the opportunity to screen projects.[12] Project evaluation procedures also call for scrutiny of the extent to which WID issues have been considered at each stage of the project cycle. The present evaluation system of ongoing projects in the UNDP provides no information on women's participation in project activities, clearly and on a systematic basis, but there have been two thematic evaluations of women's participation in UNDP activities.

Thematic evaluations are done on a selective basis as warranted, and the responsibility for the assessment is shared by the governments concerned, the UNDP, and the particular UN agency involved. In 1978, the UNDP undertook a joint agency-UNDP assessment of rural women's participation in development, proceeding by means of regional reviews,

country case studies, and a review of relevant parts of the UNDP's global
and interregional program. The results and recommendations for action
were presented to the Governing Council and to the world conference of
the UN Decade for Women at Copenhagen in 1980,[13] with the full
report issued under the title *Rural Women's Participation in Development*.
The UNDP Governing Council endorsed these recommendations, and
the UNDP administrator issued instructions to staff, including the following:

1. Training of UNDP and Agency Staff at all levels through the
incorporation of components of special relevance to women's role in
development into UNDP's staff training program.

2. Inclusion of programmes and projects of particular interest to
women in the country and inter-country-programmes; ensuring that
women are involved in all projects where their participation is desir-
able; attending to women's special requirements (e.g. training, education, health, income-generation, water supply, etc.) This would be
accomplished through a review and revision as appropriate of relevant
instructions in the Policy and Program Manual, especially those concerning project formulation, tripartite reviews, evaluation and collaboration with non-governmental organizations to ensure that women's
interests are taken into account.

3. Improved data base for the planning of women's participation
in UNDP-supported programmes and projects, especially intensive
and extensive studies on women's work situation and more comprehensive country profiles on women's situation. This is to be accomplished through the preparation of Addendum to Program Guidelines
issued in 1977, further elaborating on the subject in the light of the
findings of *Rural Women's Participation in Development*.

4. Improved flow of information to enable women's groups
around the world to become better informed of one another's activities and to permit UNDP to assess possibilities of collaboration with
such groups. To achieve this objective, UNDP would collect and dis-
tribute information on women's participation in development.

5. To continue to pay special attention to the recruitment and
training of women staff in UNDP in order to obtain a more equal distribution between the sexes at all levels.

6. To evaluate the implementation of recommended activities;
review and appraise the extent of implementation in reports to the
Governing Council.[14]

In 1985, another evaluation study, "Women's Participation in
Development: An Inter-Organizational Assessment," was presented to the
World Conference to Review and Appraise the Achievements of the
United Nations Decade for Women. The UNDP coordinated this study,
but was not included among the organizations assessed because projects

were categorized according to the agencies that either executed projects or funded *and* executed them, and the UNDP is, primarily, a funding agency. There were assessments for 215 projects operational in 1984, executed by eleven executing or participating UN agencies in four countries (Rwanda, Democratic Yemen, Indonesia, and Haiti); total budget allocation for these projects was $168,334 million. The projects were divided into four categories in terms of the inclusion of women:

Category 1   projects of exclusive concern to women
Category 2   projects designed to include women
Category 3   projects affecting women but with provision made for their direct participation
Category 4   projects of no immediate interest to women

The findings of the study show that 56 percent of projects fell in Category 3; these projects received 63 percent of the total resources. Category 4 accounted for 27 projects and commanded 0.6 percent of resources; the data for Category 2 were 12 percent of projects and 11 percent of resources. Thus, comparing the number of Category 2 projects (27) with Category 3 projects (121) shows that fewer than one in six projects reported to affect women were planned to involve them in implementation.[15] This study cited the following as the major obstacle to gender-sensitive programs and projects: "the continuing failure among United Nations organization staff to perceive the significance of women to the achievement of many national development plans, or once this is perceived a lack of experience or guidance as to how to activate the perception effectively."[16]

Programs and Projects

Project and sector activities. The UNDP has identified sixty-five country projects that were operational between 1978 and 1989 as examples involving women. These projects, meant to be illustrative rather than representative,[17] are classified in Table 2.1 by sector and geographical area. Sixty-five is a very small number of projects given that the UNDP has over five thousand projects a year, but this sample does serve to illustrate the sector and geographical areas in which women's participation is prominent, as well as the nature of women's participation.

I have divided these sixty-five projects into three categories to analyze the extent of women's participation: Type A projects affect women but make no provision for their direct participation; Type B projects are designed to include women by providing them with access and resources; and Type C projects are of exclusive concern to women, that is, women constitute the major or sole beneficiaries. Table 2.2 shows how the sixty-five projects are divided according to these categories.

Table 2.1 UNDP Projects Involving Women, by Sector and Region, 1978–1989

	East and South Africa	West Africa	Europe, Middle East, and North Africa	South Asia	East Asia and Pacific	Latin America and Caribbean	Total
Agriculture and Rural Development	5	8	4	3	1	3	24
Education	2	—	4	3	—	1	10
Population, Health, and Nutrition	2	—	1	1	—	—	4
Small-scale Enterprises	2	5	1	1	3	6	18
Technical Assistance	—	2	—	2	—	—	4
Water Supply and Urban Development	4	1	—	—	—	—	5
Total	15	16	10	10	4	10	65

Sources: Information furnished by the UNDP Division of Information and UNDP Women in Development Project Achievement Reports, June 1988 and June 1989.

Note: The classification of regions follows the World Bank's classification to facilitate comparison.

Table 2.2 Extent of Participation by Women in 65 UNDP-Funded Projects, 1978–1989

	Type A	Type B	Type C
Number	21	16	28
Percentage	32	25	43

Type A projects are those that do not provide women with special resources or access or include women in the design but that do benefit them. For example, the Burma Crop Development Project aims to increase the production of maize, pearl millet, sugarcane, sorghum, and sunflower, and thus to increase farmers' incomes. The project summary indicates that farmers' incomes have registered substantial gains, including those of most of the 4.3 million rural women in farm families who have traditionally been involved in Burma's agriculture. Another example is the Beijing Vegetable Research Center that provides technical guidelines for vegetable production; this project also provides training and extension services to commune extension workers and officials, many of whom are women, in charge of vegetable production.

Type B projects are those that provide women with resources and access. One objective of the Tihama Agricultural Extension Services Project in Yemen, to cite one project, was to provide rural women with income-earning skills and to train them to improve family nutrition and household hygiene. Another example is a Liberian self-help village development project that introduces labor-saving devices for women and provides training and credit to enable women to undertake income-earning activities.

Type C projects target women. Projects such as Organizing Mothers' Clubs and Cooperatives in Bolivia and the Women's Handicraft Centre in the United Arab Emirates enter into this category, as does a project in Indonesia aimed at the development of the productive role of women. In this case, more than 1,850 women in twelve villages have received training, equipment, and management and marketing advice that have enabled them to increase their earnings by an average of 30 percent. In Bangladesh, Women's Training Centers have provided one thousand women with skills training for income-generating activities such as weaving, sewing, fishnet making, and tinsmithing.

As shown in Table 2.2, 68 percent of the projects have either made provisions for women's participation or have directly targeted women. The rest (32 percent) are Type A projects that claim to include women but in fact do not provide for their direct participation.

Regional and interregional programs. The UNDP has provided funding for some regional and interregional programs to integrate WID issues. It provides funding for the African Training and Research Center for Women (ATRCW) of the UN Economic Commission for Africa (ECA), and the Asian and Pacific Center for Women and Development (APCWD) of the UN Economic and Social Commission of Asia and the Pacific. The ATRCW provides assistance in strengthening or creating national competencies to design and evaluate programs, in identifying sources of funds and technical assistance, and in training for women and the introduction of technological innovations to ease women's work load. The APCWD carries out research, prepares case studies, holds training workshops, and publishes materials.

Another recipient of UNDP funding is the Program for the Integration of Women in Development, launched by the ECA in 1979. This program, which operates through four coordinators of women's programs based in the four Multinational Programming and Operational Centers (MULPOC), was mandated to undertake the following activities: training and research; strengthening of national machinery; operation of subregional machinery and participation in regional structures; development of projects in the field; inclusion of the "women" component in the projects of UNDP and other agencies; and flow of information.

In addition to the program based in the MULPOCs, the UNDP finances two other projects launched and implemented by the ECA that are of direct concern to women: a project of support to the Africa Regional Coordinating Committee for the Integration of Women in Development, a regional program; and a training project on women, management, and development planning with an African perspective, a subregional project set up within the Eastern and Southern Africa Management Institute (ESAMI) at Arusha, Tanzania, and implemented jointly with the ESAMI. The regional program has a number of projects involving both action and research, relevant for the productivity of women's work: water and energy; agricultural policies; extension and technologies; the informal economy; and science and technology. Studies planned on the social consequences of structural adjustment will also include WID issues. Furthermore, the Organization of African Unity and the African Development Bank both receive support for their units for women in development.[18]

The UNDP has provided administrative and technical support for an interregional project titled Promotion of the Role of Women in Water and Environmental Sanitation Services (PROWWESS) since 1983. This project is funded by the governments of Canada, Finland, Norway, and the United States as well as by the UNDP.[19] Its objective is to involve women in water and sanitation activities by training them in participatory techniques. Demonstration projects are under way in thirteen countries in Asia, Africa, the Middle East, and Latin America and are planned in seven more. Many development agencies are involved in the execution of this project, such as the World Health Organization (WHO), the United Nations Children's Fund (UNICEF), the United Nations Development Fund for Women (UNIFEM), the Swedish International Development Agency (SIDA), the World Bank, and USAID. In Sri Lanka, the UNDP cooperates with the Women's Bureau to promote women's involvement in all phases of UNICEF-assisted water supply and sanitation improvement activities in the country's driest zone; in Zimbabwe, the project trains women volunteer health workers and supports water and sanitation improvements in commercial farm areas through Save the Children (UK); and in Kenya, the project is involved in community participation and training activities of the Kenya Water for Health Organization with UNDP, World Bank, and SIDA assistance. The project's global activities include the preparation of case studies of country experience in Asia, and a software monograph for engineers and other technical personnel, in cooperation with the World Bank Technical Advisory Group.[20]

In Asia, the Asia and Pacific Development Center receives program support for research on WID issues, programs, and projects. A special UNDP seminar on integrating women's perspectives into development planning was held at the center for UNDP staff and government and agency representatives. A special regional project in Asia is intended to translate state policies on poverty into strategies directly addressing women and to provide examples of effective initiatives. In the Arab states region, a planned series of needs assessments for women in development is expected to generate program and project proposals.[21] Finally, a project titled Women's World Banking receives support from regional as well as interregional funds.

Country programs. At the program level, according to the revised guidelines, WID issues are to be considered at the beginning of the programming exercise as well as at later stages. At the beginning of each program cycle, the resrep's role is critical in bringing WID concerns to the attention of the government by including them in the official documents, addressed to host governments, that outline UNDP priorities. Yet, according to the review of eleven country programs undertaken by the Division of Women in Development in 1989, the integration of WID issues into country programs has been minimal. In fact, even when the host country government has shown interest, the UNDP resrep has not followed up on it:

Based on the information gathered during the field and desk reviews, it becomes clear that not only the Government but also UNDP is finding it difficult to translate the idea of women's integration in development programmes into a plan of action. None of the eleven country programmes analyzed explicitly mentioned women's concerns nor took the opportunity of women's importance in a given sector or relevant activity to make projects more gender-responsive.

Most of the country programmes reviewed addressed the participation of women in their supported activities under the "special consideration" provisions of the documents. Women in development issues, the constraints experienced by women and particularly, strategies and machineries to deal with constraints were conspicuously absent. In general, there was no indication that the issue was given serious consideration or, if discussed in depth, that any possible solution had been found by those in charge.[22]

Staffing

A position for a WID officer was established within the Bureau for Policy and Program Evaluation in the late 1970s; the officer is supposed to work with the regional promoters in the headquarters. Special promoters of women's interests were designated in 1977 in each of the UNDP's four regional bureaus; they received no additional resources, but were asked to keep track of the regional bureaus' work regarding gender-sensitivity. They were supposed to assess project proposals from the point of view of women's participation and monitor and report progress.

In 1986, Draper established the Division for Women in Development within the bureau. The new division (with three professional staff members—the head of the division and two others) is responsible for seeing that women's needs and capabilities are systematically considered in projects and programming. Draper also announced the major new thrust of making one national and one international officer in each UNDP country office specifically responsible for seeing that UNDP-supported projects and programs of development in that country take women into consideration as part of their design. Furthermore, every new project presented for approval is to include an analysis of its contribution to increasing women's share and role in development.[23]

The UNDP has also organized staff training programs on WID issues. At the start of the UN Decade for Women, the UNDP produced WID courses for action, which included two motion pictures for orientation and training, as well as six sound-slide films, accompanied by discussion guides. These were distributed to all UNDP country offices with the recommendation that the materials be used to train both UNDP and other UN agency staff. The UNDP conducted one training seminar on women in development in collaboration with the World Bank, using the framework of analysis originally developed by the Bank with the assistance of the Harvard Institute of International Development. Its training program in 1980 comprised a number of courses, which mainly addressed themselves to problems of administration and management: "Only one course concerns programme management and even here there is very little emphasis on substantive aspects of programming. Techniques of project formulation and appraisal and development of managerial and decision-making skills are given major emphasis."[24]

After the Division for Women in Development was established, the number of training workshops and seminars in both New York and the field increased. These training seminars have included middle-level and senior-level management from other UN agencies such as UNICEF, UNFPA, and UNIFEM, as well as from the UNDP and host governments. The following staff training workshops and seminars have been held since 1987:[25]

1. A pilot training workshop for focal points on women in development, July 1987, at headquarters. Participants included middle-management representatives from UNDP, UNICEF, UNFPA, and UNIFEM.
2. WID orientation seminars in UNDP field offices in Malawi, Tanzania, and Zimbabwe for international and national field office staff at these locations, October 1987.
3. WID sessions in two training courses for senior and junior economists, UNDP headquarters, autumn 1987.
4. A WID session in the seminar for senior staff held at the Institute of Social Studies in The Hague, November 1987.
5. Two headquarters staff training workshops on women in development in December 1987 for middle-level and senior management.
6. Seminars on putting WID policies into operation at field offices in Bangladesh, Ivory Coast, Dominican Republic, Egypt, India, Sri Lanka, Barbados, Bolivia, Colombia, Ethiopia, The Gambia, Iraq, Jordan, Malawi, Morocco, Peru, and Uganda in January and February 1988.
7. The Joint Consultative Group on Policy's WID seminar for UNDP, UNICEF, UNFPA, and World Food Programme (WFP) senior staff and UNIFEM and government representatives, held at the ESAMI, Arusha, Tanzania, February 1988.
8. A regional seminar on women in development in planning and project implementation for UNDP, agency staff, and government counterparts at the APCWD, Kuala Lumpur, Malaysia, February

1988, and regional training seminars in Egypt and the Dominican Republic for the countries in those regions.

Besides the workshops with a specific WID focus, WID modules were introduced into the regular training programs. For example, the development seminar for senior staff held in Tokyo had a session on this issue; the training section workshop on UNDP–World Bank collaboration included a two-day module; the courses for administrative trainees included sessions on women in development; and two interregional programming workshops had WID issues on their agenda.[26]

Summary

Until 1986, there was little progress in the integration of WID concerns into UNDP activities. After the establishment in 1986 of the Division for Women in Development to serve as a focal point, much more comprehensive WID policy guidelines were developed, with several mechanisms created for implementation: The WID director participates in action committee meetings; the project review forms are a first attempt at systematically monitoring the integration of women into UNDP projects; the tripartite reviews have begun to examine projects from a WID perspective; and the project review forms are expected to serve as a baseline for future monitoring and tripartite reviews.

Country programs have not yet integrated WID issues, though some regional and interregional projects do have WID content. The most recent evaluation study found that fewer than one in six projects reported to affect women were planned to involve them in implementation.[27] A systematic evaluation of the incorporation of WID issues into all UNDP projects has not yet been undertaken, but the analysis of a sample of sixty-five projects showed that 68 percent of them contained WID content. It is, of course, not possible to make any generalizations from this sample to all UNDP projects; until the 1986 formation of the women's division, only one person was formally assigned and paid to integrate gender issues into UNDP programs and projects. UNDP field offices now have personnel who serve as focal points for WID policy implementation.

Although efforts to integrate women into UNDP activities have increased markedly since 1987, one should keep in mind that these efforts have just begun. As the report to the UNDP Governing Council indicates, country programs and projects still have work to do:

> The fact that [country] reviews clearly indicate that women have yet to be sufficiently taken into account in UNDP country programming is partly understandable, considering that most country programmes

were formulated during 1985–87, before the reinforced emphasis on women in development throughout UNDP. . . . By paying timely and informed attention to the project document's requirement for women in development considerations, UNDP projects should, in the future, be designed and implemented to integrate women in development.[28]

Explanations of UNDP's Response

Structural Factors

The development assistance regime and UNDP. The development assistance regime includes donor governments, multilateral development assistance agencies, recipient governments, nongovernmental organizations, and beneficiaries of development assistance. How these actors approach WID issues is very important because the UNDP's response to new issues is influenced by them. This is especially true because the UNDP works within a tripartite system that includes UN executing agencies and recipient governments and accords them a voice in UNDP-supported activities. Therefore, whether the host governments, donor governments, executing agencies, and other funding partners support gender issues is a key factor in explaining the UNDP's response. As the development assistance regime began to incorporate gender issues in the late 1970s and 1980s, the UNDP became more sensitized to these issues as well. The regime's increased sensitivity to women evolved as a result of the rise of an international women's movement and the many conferences held about women under UN auspices; the proliferation of scholarly activity in the new academic field of women in development in universities and research centers in the United States and around the world; and the activities (both academic and policy-relevant) of women's organizations around the world.

A crucial condition for successful formation of regimes,[29] effective leadership, was provided by the governments of Canada, the Netherlands, Norway, Sweden, Denmark, and Finland, nations that put women on the development agenda through their bilateral, multilateral, and nongovernmental aid activities. These countries are especially important for the UNDP because their leaders sit on the Governing Council and therefore have the opportunity to influence UNDP policy directly. The governments of Sweden, the Netherlands, Norway, and Denmark also are four of the top six donors of UNDP.[30] Northern European governments and Canada have been particularly interested in WID issues and have contributed funds to UNDP projects that focus on women, including the interregional PROWWESS project, and have encouraged the UNDP to integrate women into its activities.

Furthermore, twenty-three of the sample of sixty-five projects mentioned earlier are cofunded by one or more of these governments. The bilateral aid agencies of Canada, the Netherlands, and Norway also funded a high-level management training seminar on WID issues for UN agencies in December 1986 in New York, a meeting that brought together the heads of the UNDP, UNFPA, UNICEF, and WFP.

The Nordic governments and Canada have asked the UNDP to demonstrate its commitment to implementing its WID policy, indicating their dissatisfaction with the progress made so far. The WID implementation strategy submitted to the Governing Council in June 1986 contained a comprehensive statement of action but no details regarding implementation and resource allocation. Instead, the suggestion was to approach donor governments interested in WID issues for additional resources.[31] The Nordic countries expressed their displeasure at the UNDP's apparent lack of interest in institutionalizing WID policy in a speech to the Governing Council:

> We welcome the implementation strategy for UNDP as outlined in document DP/1986/14. We are in fact somewhat surprised, however, that after so many years of talking about the importance of ensuring the role of women in development, so little has been done in a systematic manner. We endorse the strategy in its totality. . . . We would, however, have expected a more detailed outline on how UNDP intends to succeed in these important tasks. . . . The Nordic countries cannot, however, accept the proposal contained in the document regarding the financing of the activities to be carried out under the strategy. . . . It is our firm conviction that the Council as well as the UNDP administration must live up to its responsibility and accept the consequences of its position. The strategy cannot be implemented unless staff time and other resources are allocated for this purpose. The Administrator must ensure that the highest possible reallocation of existing resources for these activities be made.[32]

Evidence that these countries are prepared to use their influence to promote the UNDP's implementation of WID policy appears in the draft of the UNDP's PAN on women in development:

> Many of the major donors have been re-examining their policies, procedures and mechanisms for women in development. There are indications that as they are trying to improve the efficiency of women in development in their bilateral programmes, they are also determined to make multilateral technical cooperation on women in development more effective than it has been to date. It is suggested that they may even be preparing to use performance on women in development as one of the criteria on which they will base their support to multilateral

agencies.[33]

The UNDP administrator's response to this increased pressure supports the claim that these nations exercise effective leadership:

> If one message came through more clearly than any other, it was that Council members want to see UNDP implement in full its plans for bringing half of humanity—women—fully into the development process. To succeed, our proposals require, not more rhetoric, but a strong commitment by UN Agencies, donor and recipient countries. As far as UNDP is concerned, I have already given that commitment. The Australian delegate has proposed that we identify for practical implementation two country programmes per region where we would have the active support of the Government concerned. I have asked Regional Bureau directors to give this idea their attention, and I will report to the Council on our choice of countries and any results achieved in the coming year.[34]

In short, the UNDP's response to WID has especially been influenced by the placement of WID issues on the UN agenda and by the encouragement of Northern European and Canadian governments to consider WID issues.

Many staff members I interviewed pointed out the importance of government attitudes for WID policy, and some suggested that the UNDP could do little for women in development if host governments and executing agencies were uninterested. On the average, host governments fund more than half of project budgets through cash and in-kind contributions. The UNDP's position is also weakened by the fact that recipient countries have a dominant voice in the Governing Council with respect to both policymaking and selection of the UNDP administrator. Even though the resreps are supposed to initiate the local UNDP development activities in their notes, the practice has differed: The principle of the sovereign right of governments to determine their own priorities has tended to be interpreted as giving governments responsibility to decide the specific content of country programs. This means, in effect, that the UNDP has an essentially advisory role in the programming process and is often unable to enforce standards for sector/subsector analysis, problem identification and diagnosis, and project identification and formulation.[35]

Generally, staff members perceive governments to be uninterested in WID issues; one staff member described the attitude this way:

> In a meeting in a developing country, at which I was the only woman, I asked why no one considered or mentioned women in development.

There was an uproar. The responses ranged from: "Madam, you don't really mean that, do you?" to "We have a women's ministry who pays attention to women, and that is different from development" to "We are the decisionmakers; when we have enough resources, we will see what we can do about women." In general, prejudice and ridicule are the prevalent attitudes.[36]

Unless WID policy is politically or financially attractive to recipient governments, there is little incentive for them to pay heed.[37] Further, governments tend not to include any WID component in their project proposals unless there are strong women's organizations in the country. Many staff members mentioned that governments must be held politically accountable in order for them to consider allocating resources to women out of UNDP funds.[38] In countries where strong women's organizations exist, development activities have tended to include women. For example, Honduras, Jamaica, Bolivia, and Malawi have influential women's groups and women at decisionmaking levels in government; therefore, there is more political commitment to women in development. Honduras was cited as one country in which women's activities are drawing funds because of the many economically active women's organizations. In Bolivia, mothers' clubs and cooperatives receive UNDP assistance in income-generating activities in agriculture, crafts, and marketing as well as in the organization of cooperatives and other small businesses. The Malawi government shows interest in incorporating women into its development programs, and the country has a strong national women's organization, down to the village level, that works with community workers.[39]

In general, however, government agencies that deal with women's concerns are perceived to be weak, with few resources. They are usually not implementing agencies and do not have technical expertise. In such cases, even if women are written into programs or projects as a result of the UNDP resrep's initiative, WID provisions tend to be dropped first and reallocated elsewhere if the recipient government perceives the resources as insufficient.

In some countries that are more developed, such as Greece, Turkey, and Yugoslavia, or where UNDP resources represent a "drop in the bucket," as in India, the likelihood of UNDP influence is perceived to be even lower.[40] In smaller and poorer countries, the resrep may have more leverage, but at the same time, some see an opening for executing agencies to influence the use of UNDP funds in such instances:

In countries where UNDP does have some influence on the planning process, host country governments often lack central direction and control. Consequently, executing agencies are able, through their contacts with sectoral ministries, to promote programs of interest to them, without regard necessarily to priorities established by the central planning agencies of the recipient governments and/or to UNDP program considerations.[41]

Executing agencies have the technical know-how and are responsible for managing projects. The UN General Assembly has stipulated that UNDP give priority to UN executing agencies for development activities within their sectoral emphasis and otherwise to explain why a project within an executing agency's specialized area is not given to it: "Whatever technical expertise may be called for in the process of project formulation is primarily the responsibility of the executing and participating agencies."[42]

Many UNDP staff members felt that executing agencies had a major role in implementing WID policy and that their attitude is very important. As one put it: "UNDP does overall programming, but project formulation and sector work is the responsibility of the executing agency so that the orientation of the executing agency and whether there are allies in that agency is very important."[43] UN executing agencies are generally not perceived by the UNDP staff as enthusiastic about implementing WID decisions—some even see them as the main stumbling block—but some agencies get higher marks than others. When asked which agencies show interest in women in development and are willing to cooperate, staff most often mentioned UNICEF, the International Labor Organization (ILO), and the Food and Agriculture Organization (FAO), in ascending order,[44] a perception supported by the fact that out of the sixty-five UNDP projects described earlier, twenty were executed by the FAO, eleven by the ILO, and eight by UNICEF.

UNDP's goals and procedures. The UNDP's ultimate goal is to promote self-reliance and self-determination in developing countries. As with any organizational goal, this goal rests on a particular value system, or an organizational ideology. Organizational ideologies provide beliefs about cause-and-effect relations that explain events. UNDP staff members commonly believe that the conditions in the Third World can best be explained by the problem of its political and economic dependence on external forces. Such ideological explanations provide the bases for action and understanding. Ideologies also have evaluative and prescriptive components that differentiate among alternative actions. The UNDP prescribes change strategies that will help Third World governments help themselves. Its basic guidelines include not only self-determination and self-reliance but also neutrality and respect for sovereignty. The principle of self-determination reads: "Development in each country must grow out of that country's particular needs, desires and potentialities. It is impossible to transfer a given pattern of development intact from one area to another." The principle of self-reliance says: "The proposed technical assistance activities are intended to help the underdeveloped countries to help themselves. . . . This purpose cannot be achieved unless the countries concerned are willing to take vigorous action to establish the internal conditions upon which sound development is based."[45] Ideologies also have a social consequence—they bind together individuals who share them. In the case of the UNDP, staff prides itself on being nonprescriptive and respecting the sovereignty and rights of developing countries, not imposing its version of development on them.

How does this value system affect WID policy? The emphasis on countries' right to self-determination has tended to turn the UNDP into an eclectic organization with little substantive focus. The UNDP's work encompasses virtually every aspect of economic and social development under a large number of resolutions from the UN General Assembly and/or UN global conferences that have invited specific action by the UNDP. These actions range from industrial training (GA Resolution 2090, 1965), natural resources development (GA Resolution 2158, 1966), tourism (GA Resolution 2529, 1969), and public administration (GA Resolution 2824, 1971) to integrated rural development (World Food Conference, Rome, 1974) and technical cooperation among developing countries (GA Resolution 3251, 1974).

In short, many issues besides women in development are part of the UNDP's mandate; therefore, none has any particular priority unless so declared by the UNDP and its partners (the donor and recipient governments, UN executing agencies, and NGOs). Because organizations are less inclined to accept new issues that are inconsistent with their goals—and WID issues do not constitute an integral part of the UNDP's goals—it is easy to see why the response has been relatively slow.

A basic aspect of the UNDP's procedures is the function of coordination. That the UNDP must coordinate development assistance within the decentralized tripartite system has important implications for WID policy because the UNDP's insistence alone is not sufficient for implementation. Within this system, project proposals are a government prerogative, and the technical expertise called for in the process of project formulation is primarily the responsibility of the UN executing and participating agencies.

An example of how the difficulty of coordination in a decentralized system affects gender policy comes from a report on the UNDP-ECA programs for the integration of women in development, which evaluated women's programs in the MULPOCs in Africa. This report, in concluding that no real success could be reported on the inclusion of the WID component in UNDP projects or on the flow of information between the MULPOCs, identified the following problems: (1) dual dependency of the program on the UNDP and ECA without adequately harmonizing the positions of these two organizations on essential aspects of project organization and (2) dual responsibility for the program within the ECA. The Economic Cooperation Office and the ATRCW do not always succeed in properly coordinating their instructions to the directors of the MULPOCs and the WID coordinators.[46]

The tripartite system may also encourage ambiguous definition of responsibilities, making it easy to "pass the buck" or declare a situation to be "not my problem."[47] The UNDP's relationship with UNIFEM exemplifies such a situation. In 1976, the General Assembly established the Voluntary Fund for the United Nations Decade for Women to ensure support for women in productive activities that directly assist the poor women of developing countries. UNIFEM's resources, between $3 million and $4 million annually, are derived from voluntary contributions from governments and NGOs and from a special fund. UNIFEM originally reported to the UN Division of Social and Humanitarian Affairs, then in 1986 became a UNDP-administered fund along with other special funds such as the United Nations Capital Development Fund or the United Nations Fund for Science and Technology Development.[48] The UNDP has administered some 90 percent of UNIFEM projects since 1979, and the UNDP, UN regional commissions, and UN specialized agencies provide technical and geographical support to project appraisals and execution.

It is not yet clear what the authority relationship between the UNDP and UNIFEM will be. Because of the ambiguity of UNIFEM's place in the UNDP's organizational structure, UNDP staff members lack a clear perception about how to deal with UNIFEM. One group within the UNDP wants UNIFEM to come under more direct control of the UNDP through the appointment of a UNDP staff member to oversee its activities; another group wants to let UNIFEM implement WID policy for the UNDP; yet another group sees a place for both UNIFEM and the UNDP in implementing policy. Likewise ambiguous is the division of labor regarding the supervision and implementation of UNIFEM projects by UNDP country offices. Interviews revealed that some staff members felt resentment at having to appraise UNIFEM projects or implement them without commensurate authority, a reaction that can lead to lack of attention to UNIFEM projects. At the same time, the existence of UNIFEM has led to the assumption by UNDP staff members that they do not need to be concerned with the implementation of WID policy, and this has sometimes led to ignoring women, as mentioned in an internal memo:

The Voluntary Fund for Women has too often been seen as the principal source of WID. This may have led to an unintended bias against projects the main objective of which is the promotion of women's interests by their direct participation in the design and implementation of projects. Because of the Voluntary Fund, it is not uncommon to overlook women as active participants in the mainstream of UNDP-supported development programs. The Voluntary Fund should be seen as an opportunity to further women's participation in the UNDP country programming through the provision of services and facilities that are related to UNDP projects and programs but for which IPF funds may not be available but consultant funds are available from VFDW.[49]

Since 1985, UNIFEM's mandate has been expanded to include "acting as a catalyst to promote greater participation by women in UNDP's mainstream development activities."[50] The influence of UNIFEM in the UNDP may increase as a result of this expanded mandate, which includes providing consultants to donor roundtables and participating in fund-UNDP joint programming missions and country programming exercises. The perception of UNIFEM's influence varied widely among UNDP staff members: Some indicated that UNIFEM was very effective and that they enjoyed working with it; others suggested that even though the fund is weak in programming and is dependent on the UNDP to appraise and execute its projects and to provide financial and personnel services, it pays little attention to the field offices' advice or comments; some mentioned that the staff resented doing project appraisals for UNIFEM when the fund has done no prior preparation. UNIFEM staff members, on the other hand, mentioned the difficulty of making any inroads in the UNDP and the general resistance to WID implementation.

The nature of the UNDP's procedures affects the kind of personnel hired. Because of the emphasis on coordination, UNDP personnel are first and foremost administrators. The training program for the staff centers around administrative and management issues and deemphasizes program content,[51] which means the staff does not concentrate on substantive issues (these are within the realm of UN executing agencies). The nature of the staff has several implications for gender issues: Any new issue, including WID, requires intellectual experimentation, but this type of innovation requires that one be both committed to a new issue and in a position to produce and read new research. UNDP staff members are expected neither to specialize in a particular area nor to produce research. They are receivers of new knowledge, and for WID policy, this means that the professional staff is not in a position to provide the intellectual input and the reconceptualization of development issues that are necessary for the integration of gender issues into development programs.

Constraints for WID implementation are also evident in the composition of the staff. The high-level staff members are appointed by governments, which generally appoint men who are not necessarily sensitive to gender issues. The women UNDP staff members interviewed reiterated this point, mentioning that men in high-level UNDP positions think like the men who work for developing country governments, usually come from those governments, and show a general attitude toward WID issues that has been at best disinterest and at worst ridicule. Although there is no one-to-one parallel between percentage of female professional staff and the internalization of WID policy, women professionals generally demonstrated more sensitivity to gender issues. Furthermore, in some areas of the Third World, women professionals can reach women project beneficiaries with greater ease. Some women staff members indicated that WID issues are not taken seriously by male colleagues and that the response has often been laughter when women in development was mentioned. A good example of the general attitude toward gender issues by the largely male-dominated UNDP is contained in a 1975 *UNDP News* article. A sample of staff members was asked, "What can the UNDP do on women in development issues?" Some answers follow:

What's the fuss all about? Women in Asia don't have any problems. Two Asian Prime Ministers are women.

We are already helping governments with the training of women.

African women don't want to be liberated. They are the backbone of African society.

Don't export Western problems or solutions to LDCs.

What do you mean by the integration of women into development?

Why single out women? Development is people and it is an integrated process of itself.

UNDP can do nothing unless and until governments ask us for help.

This is too controversial.

We can't do everything.

Are you prepared to go to the field?[52]

As dismaying as these responses may be, the overall attitude may be changing. The number of women on the UNDP's professional staff increased from 16 percent in 1979 to 23.6 percent in 1989.[53] Table 2.3 shows the gender breakdown of resreps.

Table 2.3 Women's Share of Management Positions in UNDP Field Offices, 1989

	Male	Female
Resreps	99	7
Interim Resreps	5	1

Source: UNDP, Division for Women in Development, internal memo, September 14, 1989.

Choice Factors: The Internal Bargaining Process

Policy-relevant activities. The structural conditions (the development assistance regime, the UNDP's goals and procedures) set the stage within which the internal bargaining process on behalf of WID issues takes place, but emphasis on the coordination of development assistance provides opportunities for UNDP staff members to act as policy entrepreneurs. Even though governments and executing agencies have considerable voice in the tripartite system, that does not exclude initiative on the part of UNDP staff members who are supportive of WID issues:

> The UNDP team in a developing country writes a resrep's note, including a conceptual framework of development planning, to the Ministry of Planning. Then the ministry convenes sectoral ministries and they have to get to work and design projects. So, UNDP can have a lot of initiative. UNDP obliges everyone to go through this process, but it doesn't always happen this way due to different circumstances. The UNDP staff can, in fact, provide input into country programs and projects; they approve or disapprove them before they can be implemented.[54]

One staff member involved in country programming in Senegal mentioned how the UNDP field office there was able to influence programming at one time. Three priority areas w ere laid out in the course of the planning, and women in development was included as a criterion in each area: "This was a strategic approach; instead of telling the government to pay attention to women in development, the UNDP staff laid out priority areas where women in development criteria was included, and the government got funding depending on whether they paid attention to these priority areas."[55] In short, those UNDP staff members who support WID issues have succeeded in integrating these concerns into projects and programs by bringing together women's organizations, governments, and UN executing agencies in particular instances.

In the headquarters, gender-sensitive staff (including those formally responsible for WID policy) have tried to integrate WID issues into agency activities through policy-relevant activities, a term that refers to influencing decisions on policy and procedures. Even though UNDP field offices have primary responsibility for country programming, the headquarters allocates funding for regional, interregional, and global programs. Those staff members sympathetic to WID concerns have taken the initiative in making sure that gender issues are not ignored in these programs. As one staff member pointed out: "In regional programs, there is a lot of scope for UNDP to take the initiative on women in development. While acting on the priorities of Third World governments, staff members also screen projects so that they are more in the driver's seat."[56] One regional program officer mentioned that she made sure that reports from executing agencies included WID concerns; if not, she rejected them. She mentioned that very few regional projects on women's activities are proposed by governments: "Among the nine hundred projects submitted by governments for the current program cycle, only two were on women. UNDP put in a project for women and it got third priority from governments. It could partly be political, but governments may also welcome the initiative from UNDP."[57] Keeping in mind that the UNDP's goals and procedures accord voice to its development partners, WID advocates in the UNDP have allied themselves with other gender-sensitive professionals within the UN system to bring about change. For example, a group of women in the UNDP, in cooperation with staff members in other UN agencies (the WFP, UNICEF, and UNFPA) and Nordic and Canadian bilateral aid agencies, held an important WID seminar in December 1986.[58]

Interviews conducted before 1987 revealed the widespread belief that there was little serious commitment from the management: "If policy was that every resident representative was required to make proposals on women in development in the resrep's note submitted to the planning procedure and then to come up with an impact report on women, then something would happen. In other words, if performance was affected, they would do something. This is a bureaucracy and people do what they are told."[59] An internal memo on WID training programs states that unless decisionmakers decide on the desirability of attention to women's issues, the staff responsible for project design and evaluation will have little motivation to build it into project design.[60] As one staff member said: "There should be procedures. With no procedures, women in development is not central to development issues. This is the responsibility of the management and there isn't sufficient commitment at the top."[61]

The picture changes with the establishment of the Division for Women in Development. The head of the division is now a senior staff member who is in a position to influence policy.

Consensus-building activities. Informal working group sessions have been established to exchange views on new experiences and approaches to WID projects.[62] The WID division organizes a series of short presentations and events highlighting WID and other gender issues, and focuses efforts toward addressing these matters in projects and programs. The WID division also publishes *Women in Development Newsletter—WIDLINK,* an in-house quarterly publication that disseminates news about country and regional experiences with project-specific issues related to women in development.

Another way to build consensus is through staff training. The division had held a total of twenty-two training workshops at the headquarters, regional, and country levels by September 1988.[63] Furthermore, the UNDP training program has begun to incorporate gender training within its standard training of program staff. Over 460 people were trained in WID/gender issues during 1988.[64]

Conclusions

As development assistance regime norms have expanded to include WID issues under the leadership of Nordic donor countries and Canada, the UNDP has been encouraged to respond more extensively to WID concerns. However, the UNDP's own goals and procedures have often acted as constraints. The UNDP's goal of coordination of technical assistance rests on a particular ideology that values self-reliance and self-determination of developing nations, and this ideology constrains UNDP personnel from experimenting with new issues without support of the developing country governments.[65] Emphasis on coordination means that recipient governments and executing agencies have to be convinced.

The decentralized tripartite system makes it easy to "pass the buck." Decisionmaking becomes very localized when outcomes depend on the particular interaction among the resrep, the recipient government, and executing agencies. However, this very tendency for local decisionmaking also encourages innovation in specific instances. Country resreps who are gender-sensitive have been able to bring together other like-minded actors within the tripartite system. For example, a resrep in Honduras was instrumental in bringing together three national women's organizations, the Dutch and Italian governments as donors, and UNIFEM to launch an experimental, and so far successful, women's income-generating project:

> In Honduras, there is an innovative project called Participation of Women in the Development Process. By using a revolving fund, loans are made to groups of women for various economic activities. The executing agency is FAO, and the government agency is the National Agrarian Institute. There is also an organization of peasant women. The women are asked what types of economic activity they want to start and are helped in preparing projects. For example, they started a successful bakery.[66]

PROWWESS, the interregional project initiated by the UNDP, is another example of successful cooperation, providing advisory and technical support by holding workshops, distributing information, and working with NGOs to ensure women's effective involvement in drinking water and waste disposal projects. Thus, the Honduras and PROWWESS examples indicate that women were incorporated into UNDP activities when a combination of actors supportive of WID concerns came together in particular projects and localities.

Since the mid-1980s, efforts at the international level to consider WID issues have increased. The development assistance regime has begun to be redefined to include women as a result of the maturation of the international women's movement, the accumulation of past experiences with women's issues, and the leadership of Nordic and Canadian donors. As more governments and UN executing agencies show interest in WID issues, the UNDP has begun to respond more actively.

Notes

1. UNDP, *Generation: Portrait of the United Nations Development Programme, 1950–1985* (New York: Division of Information, 1985), p. 12.

2. UNDP, *Women in Development—Project Achievement Reports from the UNDP* (New York: UNDP, June 1989).

3. UNDP, *A Better Environment for Development—1986 Annual Report* (New York: UNDP, 1986).

4. UNDP, "Guidelines on the Integration of Women in Development," G3100-1, 25 February 1977.

5. Ibid., p. 1.

6. Ibid., p. 2.

7. Ibid., p. 1.

8. UNDP, "Programme Implementation—Women in Development: Implementation Strategy," DP/1986/14, 26 February 1986, p. 3.

9. UNDP, Division of Women in Development, "Women in Development:

Policy and Procedures," unpublished paper, 17 November 1987.

10. Ibid.

11. UNDP, Governing Council, "Programme Implementation —Implementation of Decisions Adopted by the Governing Council at Previous Sessions: Women in Development," DP/1989/24, 15 March 1989, p. 8; these forms had not yet been analyzed at the completion of this book.

12. UNDP, Governing Council, "Programme Implementation—Decisions Adopted by the Governing Council at Previous Sessions: Women in Development," DP/1987/15, 20 April 1987.

13. UN, General Assembly, "United Nations Decade for Women: Equality, Development and Peace: Financial and Technical Support Activities of Relevant Organizations and Bodies of the United Nations System," A/36/485, 16 September 1981.

14. UNDP, "Integration of Women in Development—Implementation of Governing Council Decision 80/22/II," UNDP/PROG/79; UNDP/PROG/FIELD/120, 12 February 1981, Appendix I, pp. 1–5.

15. UNDP, *Women's Participation in Development: An Inter-Organizational Assessment*, Evaluation Study 13 (New York: UNDP, June 1985), pp. 36–43.

16. Ibid., p. 8.

17. To my knowledge, a comprehensive analysis of the inclusion of WID in all UNDP projects has not yet been undertaken. The information used to classify projects in Table 2.1 was received from the project achievement reports furnished by the UNDP Division of Information as looseleaf project reports, as well as the following UNDP publications: *Women in Development—Project Achievement Reports from the UNDP* (New York: UNDP, June 1988); and *Women in Development—Project Achievement Reports from the UNDP* (New York: UNDP, June 1989).

18. UNDP, Governing Council, "Programme Implementation—UNDP Cooperation with Non-Governmental Organizations and Grass-Roots Organizations; Women in Development—Report of the Administrator," DP/1988/15/Add.1, 11 May 1988.

19. UNDP, *Women in Development—Project Achievement Reports*, June 1989, pp. 34–37.

20. UNDP, *Is There a Better Way?* (New York: Division of Information, June 1985).

21. UNDP, DP/1988/15/Add.1, pp. 2–4.

22. UNDP, Division for Women in Development, "An Amalgamation of WID Reviews of Eleven Countries' Country Programmes," unpublished paper, June 1989, p. 16.

23. UN, "Aid Where It Works," *Development Forum* 15, 2 (March 1987): 4.

24. UNDP, "Integration of Women in Development," UNDP/PROG/79, Appendix 2, p. 1.

25. UNDP, "Programme Implementation," DP/1988/15, p. 16; "Programme Implementation," DP/1989/24.

26. UNDP, "Programme Implementation," DP/1989/24.

27. UNDP, *Women's Participation in Development*, pp. 36–43.

28. UNDP, "Programme Implementation," DP/1989/24, pp. 5, 11.

29. Young, "Politics of International Regime Formation," p. 373.

30. The other two are the United States and Japan.

31. UNDP, "Programme Implementation," DP/1986/14.

32. UNDP, Governing Council, "Statement by Denmark on behalf of the Nordic Countries," 33d Sess., 12 June 1986, pp. 3–4.

33. UNDP, Bureau for Programme and Policy Evaluation, Technical Advisory Division, "Draft UNDP Programme Advisory Note: Women in Development," unpublished paper, May 1986, p. 5.

34. UNDP, Governing Council, "Response by William H. Draper III," 33d Sess., 12 June 1986, p. 3.

35. Patrick Demongeot, "U.N. System Development Assistance," *U.S. Foreign Assistance: Investment or Folly?* eds. John Wilhelm and Gerry Feinstein (New York: Praeger, 1984), pp. 318–319.

36. UNDP interviews, New York, June 1986.

37. See, e.g., Jeffrey Pressman and Aaron Wildavsky, *Implementation* (Berkeley: University of California Press, 1973); and Martha Derthick, *New Towns In Town* (Washington, DC: Urban Institute, 1972). Both books discuss the tensions between recipients and donors of funds.

38. UNDP interviews, New York, June 1986.

39. Ibid.

40. Ibid.

41. Demongeot, "U.N. System Development Assistance," p. 317.

42. UNDP, "Integration of Women in Development," UNDP/PROG/79.

43. UNDP interviews, New York, June 1986.

44. Ibid.

45. UNDP, *Generation.*

46. UNDP, "Report of the Mission to Evaluate the UNDP/ECA Programs for the Integration of Women in Development, 7 May–7 July 1984," unpublished paper, p. ii.

47. See Bardach, *Implementation Game.*

48. UN, General Assembly, Resolution A/RES/39/125, 14 December 1984.

49. UNDP memorandum from the administrator to UN executing agencies, UNDP headquarters staff and field offices, 14 September 1982.

50. UN, General Assembly, A/RES/39/125.

51. UNDP, "Integration of Women in Development," UNDP/PROG/79, Appendix 2.

52. UNDP, "Female Imperatives in Development," *UNDP News* (January-February 1975): 15–16.

53. UNDP, internal memorandum, 1989.

54. UNDP interviews, New York, June 1986.

55. Ibid.

56. Ibid.

57. Ibid.

58. UN, *Equal Time,* published by the Group on Equal Rights for Women in the United Nations (double midyear issue, 1987): 7.

59. UNDP interviews, New York, June 1986.

60. UNDP, internal memorandum, 1986.

61. UNDP interviews, New York, June 1986.

62. *Equal Time* (midyear issue, 1987): 6.

63. UNDP, *Women in Development News—WIDLINK* (September 1988): 4.

64. FAO, The Women in Agricultural Production and Rural Development Service, "Training in WID/Gender Analysis in Agricultural Development: A Review of Experiences and Lessons," unpublished paper, July 1989, p. 13.

65. UNDP interviews, New York, June 1986.

66. Ibid.

3

Economic Rationality
and the World Bank

The World Bank encompasses the International Bank for Reconstruction and Development and its affiliates, the International Development Association and the International Finance Corporation. The common objective of these institutions is to help raise standards of living in developing countries by channeling financial resources from developed countries to the developing world. The Bank's charter spells out certain basic rules that govern its operations: It must lend only for productive purposes and must stimulate economic growth in the developing countries where it lends; it must pay due regard to the prospects of repayment; each loan is made to a government or must be guaranteed by the government concerned; and the decision to lend must be based on economic considerations.[1] In 1989, the Bank's lending reached $18 billion.

The Bank, whose capital is subscribed by its member countries, finances its lending operations primarily by borrowing in the world capital markets. A substantial contribution to the Bank's resources also comes from its retained earnings and the flow of repayments on its loans. For capital subscriptions, the Bank distinguishes between "paid-in" and "callable" capital. Each country joining the Bank is assigned a capital subscription after consultation between the Bank and the applicant and approval by the Bank's Board of Governors. Upon joining, the country pays in 10 percent of its subscription: 1 percent in gold or US dollars and 9 percent in the country's currency. The remaining 90 percent of its subscription is callable, subject to being called by the Bank if the funds are required to meet Bank obligations for loans or to guarantee loans.[2]

Established in 1945, the World Bank is owned by 151 member countries. Each member receives 250 votes plus one additional vote for each share of stock it holds, a formula that gives the United States the largest number of votes. The World Bank is situated in Washington, DC, and its president is always a US citizen. All powers of the Bank are vested in a Board of Governors, which consists of one governor appointed by each member country. With the exception of certain powers specifically reserved to them by the Articles of Agreement, such as decisions on membership, allocation of net income, and changes in the capital stock, the governors have delegated their powers to a Board of Executive Directors who meet regularly at the Bank's headquarters. Five of these directors are appointed by the five largest stockholders (France, Japan, the United Kingdom, West Germany, and the United States), and the remaining sixteen are elected by the other members.[3] The executive directors meet under the chairmanship of the president of the Bank. In practice, they reach most of their decisions by consensus; formal votes are rare. The executive directors are formally responsible for the general operations of the Bank, for deciding Bank policy, and for all loan and credit proposals.[4] In reality, however, the executive directors seem to have relatively less power than the management.[5] As Ayres suggests:

> The Bank was very much a management-run institution. This was despite the fact that the directors were required to approve every commitment of funds for development projects, as well as major changes in Bank policy. . . . But the directors' approval of these things was more or less a formality. In practice, projects were approved by the operational management of the Bank and ratified by the directors. During the course of this research for this study, no single instance was discovered of a project's being turned down by the directors. Management also had great flexibility in determining what matters of general policy it would submit to the directors for review.[6]

Structurally, the Bank is a centralized institution, with approximately 94 percent of the professional staff located in its headquarters. There is, however, an increasing trend toward establishing more resident missions; the number reached forty-three (in forty-one developing countries) in 1989, and there are three regional missions (in East Africa, West Africa, and Thailand) and offices in New York, Paris, Geneva, and Tokyo.[7] The vast bulk of the Bank's most important decisions still come from the missions that periodically visit the developing member countries.

Until 1987, the management was made up of the president, senior vice-presidents for operations and finance, vice-presidents, and division chiefs. Under the senior vice-president for operations were six vice-presidents who presided over regional offices, designated for Eastern and Southern Africa; Western Africa; East Asia and Pacific; South Asia; Europe, Middle East, and North Africa; and Latin America and Carribean. Under each regional vice-president were country programs and projects departments. Project departments were responsible for the design and appraisal of specific projects, while country programs departments oversaw development of Bank–government relations concerning the Bank's portfolio or projects in one or a few countries. The departments under the vice-president for operations policy, on the other hand, were staff units, the functional units that included the departments dealing with projects policy; country policy; agriculture and rural development; education and training; population, health, and nutrition; transportation; water supply and urban development; and the Economic Development Institute (EDI). The operations policy staff was responsible for reviewing, on a continuing basis, the Bank's functional policies and programs in the sectors to which it lends. It was involved in the project cycle of identifying, appraising, and supervising project work, and in advising, monitoring, research, or other support capacities. Staff members were charged with using their expertise in a particular substantive area to provide intellectual input into the Bank's work. These functional units were designed to check and balance the country programs and projects staff.

In 1987, the Bank was reorganized and a number of changes were introduced. The number of vice-presidents who oversee regional operations was reduced to four, and the regional offices now consist of Africa; Asia; Europe, Middle East, and North Africa; and Latin America and Caribbean. Under each of these regional offices are regional departments. For example, the Africa regional office has six regional departments: Occidental and Central Africa; Eastern Africa; South-Central and Indian Ocean; Western Africa; Sahelian; and South Africa. These regional departments no longer have separate country programs and projects departments. A further change is the setting up, under each regional office, of technical departments to address the following areas: trade, finance, and public sector; agriculture; industry and energy; infrastructure; population and human resources; and environment. Environment is a new issue that had not previously been addressed by the regional offices.

With the reorganization of the Bank, Operations Policy was renamed Policy, Planning, and Research (PPR). PPR staff is now divided into departments for international economics, country economics, agriculture and rural development, environment, infrastructure and urban development, industry and energy, population and human resources, and the EDI. Education and training issues now come under the Population and Human Resources Department (human resources is a new addition to the concerns of this department). Transportation, instead of being a separate department, is now included under the new Infrastructure and Urban Development Department. The new Environment Department has been added to the PPR staff. Until the reorganization in 1987, the Bank had an adviser on women in development housed within Operations Policy; after 1987, a Division for Women in Development was formed under the Population and Human

Resources Department within PPR.

The Bank's activities take place on a number of different levels.[8] Its goal is to be a leading institution in development theory and practice. The annual addresses of its president, the sector policy papers on development issues, the annual *World Development Report,* and its general research program are important development documents. On a second level of the Bank's work are the country dialogues, the Bank's country economic work. Best known are the economic reports on individual borrowing countries, which analyze macroeconomic performance and provide a frame of reference for subsequent Bank operations in the country, particularly at the project level. The third aspect of the Bank's work involves funding of development projects. The project cycle consists of identification, preparation, appraisal, negotiation, and supervision. Project work includes two major activities: field missions and the preparation of reports. Identification missions, which frequently include the staff of other international development agencies, try to identify promising projects or stimulate their development. Preparation of a project covers all the steps necessary to bring a project to the point at which its technical, economic, financial, social, and organizational feasibilities have been established and it is ready for appraisal.[9] The formal appraisal of a project is undertaken by a mission to the field. Once a project has been negotiated and approved, its implementation is overseen by supervision missions, detailed at least every nine months or more frequently in the case of active projects.

Response to WID Issues

Policy and Procedures

The *Operations Manual* of the World Bank is the major reference document for staff members. In January 1984, guidelines on women in development appeared for the first time in this manual under "Sociological Aspects of Project Appraisal." These guidelines were drafted by the WID adviser in cooperation with an informal group of staff members who meet and discuss sociological issues in the Bank's work. It is pointed out in this section of the manual that women, along with other specific target groups, such as resettled populations and minorities, should receive attention in project design:

> Women are sometimes a particularly important group of project participants and beneficiaries. Appraisal should therefore determine whether the project design takes into account adequately a) the local circumstances that impede or encourage the participation of women;

b) the contribution that women could make to achieving the project's objectives; c) the changes which the project will introduce that might be disadvantageous to women; and d) whether the implications for women are included in the provisions for monitoring the impact of the project.

The World Bank's *Annual Report* 1984 states that the Bank's approach to WID concerns is to try to ensure that staff members are aware of the roles of women that are relevant to the project's objectives. Staff members are asked to tailor projects in order to

1. Prevent effects that are detrimental to women; for example, where granting individual title to land discriminates against women.
2. Create opportunities for women to participate and share in project benefits; for example, by making appropriate provisions within loans and credits for the generation of income.
3. Respond to women's needs and make use of their capacities; for example, by recognizing the particular health problems of women and by upgrading the skills and status of traditional female health personnel.
4. Address the problems posed by potential limitations on women's access to funds and services; for example, by recognizing that in certain cultures, services must be delivered within the narrow sphere of relationships permitted to women.

Guidelines drafted in 1989 emphasize some key issues in economic and sector work:

1. Women already contribute economically far more than is usually recognized in official GNP statistics, particularly through agriculture, home-based production, and care of the family.

2. Women's capacity to work is often particularly constrained—and their productivity reduced—by culture and tradition, both of which are sometimes codified into law and policy. Culture and tradition, for instance, may limit their access to information and technology, to education and training, to credit and resources, and to markets.

3. Investing in women is often a cost-effective route to broader development objectives such as improved economic performance, reduction of poverty, greater family welfare, and slower population growth.

4. Women tend to be disproportionately represented among the poor.

5. When women's productive capacity is constrained, it is important not merely to "get the prices right"—to establish appropriate

incentives—but also to improve women's capacity to respond, through investment programs and policy changes, especially in agriculture, home-based production, and the small-scale or informal sector.

6. Labor markets in industry, but also in agriculture and services, are often segmented by gender, with women typically concentrated in fewer, more traditional, and less remunerative lines of work.

7. Investments in human capital for women have a high payoff, but women and girls often get less than men and boys when the costs to families of education, health care, and even food are high.

8. Improving opportunities for women can lead to more effective use of natural resources.

9. The most effective combination of measures for reducing birth rates includes expanded income-earning opportunities and education for women, in conjunction with family planning programs and health care.[10]

These guidelines are meant to help Bank staff to identify issues concerning women in country economic and sector work as well as in project design. Sector-specific guidelines have been produced for forestry,[11] and guidelines for agricultural extension and credit and for education are under way. The guidelines for forestry include issues to address during both project preparation and project supervision; how to analyze project costs and benefits with women in mind; and how to design specific forestry interventions.

Programs and Projects

Project activities. Are WID issues included in the Bank's project work—that is, in the project identification, appraisal, negotiation, supervision, implementation, and evaluation stages? The WID adviser has not been systematically involved in project identification; the projects staff plays the pivotal role at this stage. Staff members mentioned in interviews that the consideration of women in development depends very much on the individual discretion of the project officer: "New projects that are identified are usually follow-ups to old projects or spin-offs from old projects. Usually it is a personal decision so that the individual project officer decides whether, for example, there will be a health component to a project. Even though there are guidelines, there is a lot of discretion."[12] The first WID adviser once pointed out that if she happened to hear about missions going out, she would call the relevant people and suggest possible issues to consider.

The WID office does, however, review projects at the preparation and appraisal stages and can bring up problems with projects it reviews; those projects cannot advance before these criticisms are addressed.

Table 3.1 Project Appraisal Reports Reviewed by the World Bank WID Office, by Sector and Region, 1979–1984

	East and South Africa	West Africa	Europe, Middle East, and North Africa	South Asia	East Asia and Pacific	Latin America and Caribbean	Total
Agriculture and Rural Development	29	33	20	18	14	28	142
Education	24	11	21	6	6	11	79
Industry and Energy	1	2	1	3	—	1	8
Population, Health, and Nutrition	1	4	4	6	10	6	31
Technical Assistance	—	1	—	—	—	—	1
Water Supply and Sewerage	4	2	1	1	—	1	9
Water Supply and Urban Development	8	3	3	4	3	11	32
Total	67	56	50	38	33	58	302

Source: Information furnished by the World Bank, Adviser on Women in Development, May 1986.

Between 1979 and 1984, the WID office reviewed 302 project appraisal reports that addressed WID issues in six different sectors: agriculture and rural development; education; urban development and water supply; population, health, and nutrition; water supply and sewerage; and energy.[13] The other sectors in which the Bank makes project loans are development finance companies, industry, small-scale enterprises, telecommunications, and transportation. It should be noted, however, that many projects include activity in more than one sector or subsector. Appraisal reports are key in the Bank's project work, because all future work on the project—from supervision to evaluation after project completion—is carried out in terms of the recommendations contained in them. The Bank approves approximately 250 projects a year; thus, the number of projects with significant WID components compiled by the WID adviser constituted approximately 24 percent of all projects during the 1979–1984 period. Mentioning women in one way or another in project appraisal reports does not, of course, mean that these recommendations were exactly followed in implementation, and there is no way to know what actually happened in the implementation of each of these projects.

Table 3.1 serves to illustrate certain characteristics of projects with WID components: First, the two sectors with the highest number of projects having WID components are agriculture and rural development, and education; second, in terms of geographical spread, the highest number of projects that include women are located in Africa. This sample of projects is classified in Table 3.2 in terms of the nature of women's participation. I have divided the circumstances under which women are considered in appraisal reports into three types: A, in which women are mentioned as "natural" or "automatic" beneficiaries; B, in which special arrangements are made to ease women's access to project benefits (such as when women are offered education, training programs, or credit); and C, in which women constitute the major group of beneficiaries (more than 50 percent) in the whole project or a particular activity under the project.

Table 3.2 Extent of Participation by Women in 302 World Bank Projects, 1979–1984

	Type A	Type B	Type C
Number	138	127	37
Percentage	46	42	12

According to Table 3.2, 46 percent of the projects mentioned that women will participate because they are natural beneficiaries, along with men and children; in other words, women would benefit automatically.

For example, a rural development project stated that women would benefit because the project aimed at improvement of home gardens, improvement of family nutrition, community participation, training courses, and adaptive trials at the home gardens. Another agricultural project, in the Philippines, would benefit women as a result of the treatment and prevention of anemia and diarrhea. Appraisal reports on education projects in this category mention that women will benefit from improvements made in primary education as a result of more teachers and textbooks. Eleven projects in urban development and water supply mention that women will benefit because of the provision of primary schools, credit, community participation centers, water supply, and day care. Nine project appraisal reports in the area of population, health, and nutrition claim to benefit women because they provide nutrition education, family planning clinics, maternal and child health care, and day-care facilities.

Provisions that allow women access to resources existed in 42 percent of projects. One example is an agricultural extension project in Thailand in which plans call for home extension agents to visit women's groups to teach information on vegetable gardens, fruit production, food preparation and preservation, and home economics; the intent is that 15–25 percent of extension agents be women. Another example is an agricultural project in Ethiopia in which extension programs are designed with attention to the training needs of women, to women's income generation, as well as health care, child care, and birth control. A primary education project in Bangladesh provides free uniforms for girls as a way to encourage parents to send them to school and 50 percent of new primary school teaching posts are reserved for women. In Nepal, free education and free hostels are provided for women up to the secondary level; thirty spaces out of four hundred are reserved for women to be trained in agricultural and animal science.

Eighteen project reports in the area of population, health, and nutrition indicate planning of specific resources directed at women, such as incentive funds for reduced fertility; training of traditional birth attendants, paramedics, and nurses; and training in vocations for women. For example, a project on Malaysia aims to improve the socioeconomic status of women in order to give them alternatives to childbearing by setting up experimental community service centers and by training women as village community workers.

The appraisal report of an energy project in Sri Lanka states:

Women work in construction. The project would train new entrants in basic construction skills and also train experienced construction workers [two levels at which women workers seemed to be in significant numbers]. The government of Sri Lanka agreed that trainee selection for the project would be undertaken according to criteria that would encourage the participation of women in training courses at least in proportions similar to those of their participation in the industry's labor force. Cooperation of Sri Lanka's Women's Bureau would be obtained.

Twelve percent of the project appraisal reports cite women as primary or major beneficiaries. An example of such a case is a basic agricultural services project in Lesotho; because 50–60 percent of the male labor force migrates to work in South Africa, major beneficiaries will be women. Another is an integrated rural development project in Burundi through which five social centers would be upgraded; 75 percent of the students in these centers are women attending courses on home economics, sewing, and cooking.

Seven urban development and water supply projects cite women as major beneficiaries. In Thailand, for instance, the small-scale business component of a project would provide employment opportunities for about fifteen hundred residents, primarily women, who wish to work within the community and who would be unable to find employment otherwise. In Botswana, a project provides for vending shelters and low-cost industrial areas for small-scale entrepreneurs. As the report indicates, women predominate among traders who will want to rent at the low-cost commercial site. Preference will be given to women in making loans, and monitoring and evaluation would include analyzing the opportunity for women to obtain formal and informal employment.

In the population, health, and nutrition sector, three appraisal reports indicate women to be the primary beneficiaries. A project in São Paulo, Brazil, provides for a basic health unit and hospital and for training of hospital personnel, who are primarily women. A project in population education in Pakistan would promote programs for women's groups and provide for skill development or income-generating activities for women.

In the industry sector four projects provide women access to resources. The Yemen Arab Republic would conduct a study on women's employment to see if they can find jobs in administration and the textiles industry. In Bangladesh, women extension workers would be trained to work within the small-scale jute industry, a recommendation made in the appraisal report because "women are involved in handicraft production using jute; women could earn much more if marketing and production organization was introduced. In addition, expansion could build on a larger production base if training was introduced."

In short, of the 302 World Bank projects that claim to involve women (see Table 3.2), 164 (or 54 percent) specifically provide access for women by making special provisions or focus on women as the major beneficiaries. Given that the Bank approved about 250 projects per year between 1979 and 1984, 164 projects represents 13 percent of all projects during that period.

The Bank's WID division compiled a sample of twenty-five projects with significant WID components, approved between 1987 and 1989, and this sample illustrates some of the changes in the treatment of women's issues in project appraisal reports since 1984.[14] As can be seen in Table 3.3, sectors with WID components have not changed significantly compared with earlier years, and the majority of these projects are located in Africa, as before. However, the percentage of projects in this sample (see Table 3.4) that either target women or provide them with access and resources is significantly higher than in the previous sample. The implication is that projects no longer assume women will benefit automatically and are increasingly making specific provisions for their participation.

Table 3.3   World Bank Projects with WID Components, 1987-1989

Sectoral Breakdown		Regional Breakdown	
Agriculture and Rural Development	10	East and South Africa	6
Education	5	West Africa	5
Industry and Energy	4	Europe, Middle East, and North Africa	4
Infrastructure and Urban Development	1	South Asia	6
Population, Health, and Nutrition	5	East Asia and Pacific	3
		Latin America and Caribbean	1

Source: Information furnished by the World Bank, Division of Women in Development, 1989.

Table 3.4   Extent of Participation by Women in 25 World Bank Projects, 1987–1989

	Type A	Type B	Type C
Number	3	17	5
Percentage	12	68	20

How are WID issues considered in the negotiation, supervision, and evaluation stages? There is no systematic way in which these issues surface during negotiations between Bank missions and borrower governments; they may or may not be raised by either party. An earlier case in which a WID issue was made part of a loan agreement involved a population, health, and nutrition project in the Dominican Republic. The agreement included the training of nurses as part of the project and stipulated that the salary structure of nursing personnel would be periodically reviewed to give them incentive to remain in the profession. Supervision is the weakest link in the Bank's project work; there is no continuous supervision because the majority of the Bank staff is in the headquarters. Thus, the inclusion of WID issues in appraisal missions and reports is not an automatic guarantee that implementation will reflect them. Appraisal reports are, however, important guidelines that are used in the evaluation process.

Evaluation of the Bank's project work is done by the Operations Evaluations Department, which reports directly to the Board of Executive Directors. This independent unit within the Bank conducts reviews, on a selective basis, of Bank-supported projects, programs, and operational policies and attempts to determine whether they are realizing their objectives and how they might be made more effective, efficient, and responsive to the needs and concerns of member countries.

Agricultural research and extension is an area in which women are considered relevant, yet evaluation of projects points out that recognition of women's role has been poor at the operational level:

> For example, in India's Sixth Five-Year Plan, considerable attention was given to women's role in agriculture. More agricultural extension and training resources were to have been allocated for women farmers. However, not one female agricultural extension worker was encountered during the mission to India. Even in a sericulture project in the southern state of Karnataka where women have been largely involved with silk production and processing, there was no mention of women in the project reports, nor of the need to have women extension workers. A small pilot project in Karnataka funded by the Ford Foundation has involved female extension workers in sericulture; it appears to be quite successful. The situation is not very different in other countries, except in Thailand. In Thailand, 14 percent of the field-level extension agents are women, and women are represented at all professional levels of the extension system. Among the Bank project documents reviewed, many included recommendations that facilitated access by women farmers to extension services. Such recommendations, however, needed to be translated into specific programs, particularly in training women extension staff.[15]

So far, no study has been done to evaluate the Bank's experience with women in development. At the end of each year, project performance audit reports are collectively reviewed and the results organized into a single report. The *Tenth Annual Review of Project Performance Audit Results 1984* "synthesizes and critically examines the experience of over one thousand projects whose results have been evaluated over the last ten years." This report mentions women in the section on agriculture under the subheading "Suitability of Technology": "Sometimes new technologies which were capable of providing much higher yields were found unattractive because they gave an inadequate return to the farmers' labor, or involved too much risk, or failed to take account of sociological issues, such as the roles of men and women in production or attitudes toward communal production systems."[16] The 1985 annual review mentions that in education, some project components were aimed primarily at women: "For example, 90% of the adults in the rural education centers in one project were women; there was high female participation in a mass media project; and two primary teacher training colleges especially for women were included in another project." The report points out that "efforts at promoting female participation in education need to be vigorously pursued in view of the importance women have in size of family, nutrition and health."[17]

More recently, an evaluation study has considered how women in three West African countries have been affected by the introduction there of cotton:

[W]omen are accorded limited or declining access to land for crops which may lead to an income, despite their desire to have such plots. Increasingly, they contribute substantially in terms of their labor to all aspects of agricultural production, not just the traditional sowing and harvesting, but they receive inadequate extension. Overall benefits from cotton have been inequitably distributed in that revenues have frequently been used to increase the incidence of polygamy, which women resent. In some cases, women's overall financial independence has deteriorated while little has improved in respect of their traditional and time-consuming activities of child care, food preparation, and wood and water collection. To a certain degree, the introduction of cotton has enabled the power of households to become consolidated. Remedial action in respect of the status of women and children will require, therefore, greater awareness on the part of men, through training, of the importance of more equitable involvement of women in agricultural production. Governments can assist this as an important issue. Encouraging female school attendance may be an additional remedy.[18]

Sector activities. The major sectors in which the staff's work has included women are population, health, and nutrition; education and training; agriculture and rural development; and water supply and sanitation.[19] The Bank's initial interest in the role of women was in the area of population, health, and nutrition. An examination of the 1978 and 1984 abstracts of current studies reveals that most research related to women has been in this field and directed toward understanding the determinants of fertility.[20] My research reveals that the first activity related to women that drew Bank participation was the International Forum on the Role of Women in Population and Development held in 1974.[21] Bank studies have demonstrated that maternal and child health care and better employment and education opportunities for women are related to a decline in fertility.[22]

The 1984 report indicates that in all countries, women who have completed primary school have fewer children than do women with no education, and everywhere the number of children declines regularly as the education of mothers increases above the primary school level.[23] There have also been a number of studies done by staff members and consultants on the relationship between education and fertility, which have found evidence of correlations between fertility and the situation of women.[24] The lower the level of education, the higher the rate of fertility; the lower the threshold of economic well-being, the higher the rate of fertility; the greater the likelihood of an urban residence, the lower the rate of fertility; and the higher the labor force participation of women, the lower the rate of fertility. The Bank's 1984 report has a section on women's employment and status that argues that decline in fertility is associated both with increased development and with increased status for women.[25] The EDI has also produced a number of studies on education and women, one of which analyzed gender concerns in educational issues in Arab countries.[26] Another study on women and vocational education in different regions is intended as an input into the world conference on education to be held in 1990.

This emphasis has continued with the appointment of Barbara Herz as the new WID adviser in 1985. Herz has indicated that she will focus on population, health, and nutrition, along with agriculture and employment. One of her theme initiatives is safe motherhood, aimed at providing maternal health and family planning services at the local level. This initiative led to a senior-level conference in Nairobi, Kenya, in February 1987, sponsored by the World Bank, the UNFPA, and the WHO. The participants included members of the donor community; multilateral, bilateral, and nongovernmental organizations such as the USAID, SIDA, and the Ford and Rockefeller foundations; and senior government officials of developing countries.[27] The two background papers for this safe motherhood conference were published by the Bank.[28]

In the sector of agriculture and rural development, the 1975 policy paper mentions women in relation to training and research. This document cites a staff working paper on rural poverty and nonformal education and draws particular attention to "the need for greater equity to avoid widening the socioeconomic gap in rural areas. Worthy of particular note is the neglect of training for women, although the importance of their roles in making decisions and doing farm work is acknowledged."[29] Two staff working papers have also focused on the role of women in the agricultural sector in Bangladesh and Nepal.[30]

The WID office produced a sectoral review on forestry projects and women in September 1980, reviewing forty-three projects for issues related to women's involvement in forestry and wood-using activities and finding that nineteen had included women.[31] The report's criterion for the inclusion of women in projects is a combination of specific reference to women; social community; rural forestry components; use of agricultural residue and dung as fuel; promotion of increased use of charcoal; introduction of alternative fuels; introduction of improved stoves; local participation in project implementation; extension services; and training, research, and studies. This report recommended that women be trained as interviewers for forestry-related surveys and approached as informants and that efforts be made to involve women in project activities through their participation and training.

Herz has proposed to focus on agriculture and rural development, specifically agricultural extension services and credit, as one of the important sectors for women. She has indicated that an effort "to assess experience, identify promising approaches and perhaps highlight some cases" will be made with the cooperation of the Agriculture and Rural Development Department and the regional offices.[32] A WID task force at the EDI also works with Herz to develop case studies for use in courses on women in agriculture.

Water supply and sanitation is another sector in which women's issues have been considered. A staff report points out that because women are the primary users of water and sanitation systems and have principal influence on family sanitary habits, they have much to contribute to the better planning, functioning, and utilization of improved facilities: "Women's involvement in water supply and sanitation projects is not simply as beneficiaries, i.e. merely profitting from the time and energy saved or the health improvement gained from the new or improved facilities. . . . The Bank should exercise leadership in helping women's share in development to improve the efficiency of its total development efforts."[33] The same paper suggests that women should be trained and supported for higher levels of involvement in their communities and that Bank strategies should be based on country-level experience. It points out that more than half of the improved water and sanitation facilities in rural areas in Latin America are unused or inoperative within a few years of their installation, a result in part attributable to lack of understanding of the socioeconomic conditions that influence acceptance, rejection, or misuse of improved systems. Because women are involved with water and sanitation issues in the family, they have to be consulted:

In Honduras, for instance, a sanitation project initially failed because the latrines were used as bean storage areas. Nevertheless, the project succeeded when the project engineer discovered after meeting with village women, that they felt going to the latrine was a private function and since the walls of the latrine did not cover their feet, they refused to use it. In the Dominican Republic, a very high percentage of the hand pumps installed were breaking down. Investigation showed that the pump handles were designed for men when, in fact, women and children were the main users. Because they needed a lower pump handle position, they used the pumps inefficiently causing damage and eventual breakdown. Had the women been consulted, they could have helped to develop a design that would have made the pumps easier to use.[34]

Finally, the report ends with a checklist to help staff be more sensitive not only to the participation of women in projects but to their involvement in setting project objectives, to the consideration of constraints on women, to increasing women's access to project benefits, to being aware of women's needs, to creating opportunities for female participation in project management positions, and to the involvement of women in the collection and interpretation of data.

As part of the International Drinking Water Supply and Sanitation Decade sponsored by the United Nations, the Bank and the UNDP are cooperating in a program to conduct research in and demonstrate lower-cost approaches to water supply and sanitation technologies. This technical assistance program is active in thirty-five countries and operates at a level of $7 million a year with funding from the UNDP, UNICEF, ten bilateral donors, and several Bank borrowers. In connection with this project, PROWWESS was established and is currently active in twenty countries; its activities include participating with other donors in sector reviews and project-planning activities and providing technical assistance in the implementation of projects, especially through training in participatory methodology.[35] The project works this way in Kenya:

> Together with UNIFEM, PROWWESS has been supporting the Kenya Water for Health Organization (KWAHO) in mobilizing communities for self-help in the coastal Kwale District. Twenty-four women community leaders have been trained to maintain and repair handpumps under Government/UNDP/World Bank/SIDA rural handpump projects. They and others are organizing village water committees, discussing their own responsibilities with those installing the system and deciding where water points should be placed. They also decide on systems for collecting water fees, which are used for the purchase of spare parts and major repairs. Many of the groups which have been formed are now initiating income-generating activities.[36]

With the support of this project, the Bank has published a discussion paper about involving women in such activities.[37] Other Bank publications on water supply and sanitation also stress the importance of community participation and the role of women.[38]

In the urban development sector, women have generally not received as much attention as they have in the other areas discussed here. A number of studies were undertaken at the EDI to analyze housing issues as they relate to women.[39] Some Bank staff working papers have focused on women's economic participation in urban development.[40]

Country programs. Women are not systematically considered in country studies and country economic reports, although they are being included in reports on countries where women's economic roles are recognized (such as Nigeria and The Gambia) or where women head families and men are employed elsewhere (such as Lesotho and Yemen). Women's economic participation at the country level is one of the theme initiatives of the WID division chief, who proposed to undertake WID country strategies for two countries:

> A WID country strategy would examine the situation of women in the country and their relevance for the country's development strategy. It would suggest how to assist the country's women, to increase their contribution to its development, and would offer focused recommendations for action in key sectors. The strategy would be prepared in a close collaboration with the country concerned. It would be based on our CPPs [Country Program Papers] and economic and sector work, the country's own plans and project experience, plus some special analysis on women's issues. It would influence our future advice and lending—and hopefully prove useful to the country and other donors. At the request of Netherlands, which chairs the donor consortium for Indonesia, we prepared such a paper last year—a pioneering effort well received by the Government of Indonesia and donors. But we need to put in enough resources to be more thorough and analytic.[41]

The report Herz mentions describes the economic and social situation of Indonesian women and suggests ways in which the government and development agencies could consider WID issues and then incorporate them into the design of development projects. Some of the recommendations include setting up orientation programs for government and agency personnel; establishing an adequate data base on women; promoting economically viable opportunities for women to earn income through training and assistance with organization management, administration, credit, and marketing support; establishing WID centers in universities and institutes; and integrating the activities of NGOs in the development process, thus strengthening their capabilities.[42]

In early 1986, a mission to Kenya was undertaken to develop a country strategy on women in development. This is the first such mission to produce a strategy paper suggesting ways to strengthen development programs in several sectors. Ideas for more effective inclusion of women included expansion of agricultural extension services and credit for women to improve agricultural productivity; development of a safe motherhood initiative to reduce maternal mortality and encourage family planning; selection of six to ten model projects in agriculture, education, and population, health, and nutrition to test methods of involving women in projects on a larger scale.[43]

In 1989, Barber Conable, president of the World Bank, asked the regional departments within the four regional offices to produce a WID country strategy paper on a country of their choice within their region. As a result, WID country strategy papers have been produced on seventeen countries, including Indonesia, Ethiopia, Malawi, India, Bangladesh, Pakistan, and Yemen.

Staffing

Responsiveness to a new issue is reflected not only in the content of an organization's work but also in what resources and responsibility are allocated to the new area. In 1977, the World Bank appointed a woman from Jamaica, a former UN official, as adviser on women in development. The adviser's duties were defined as to assist in focusing attention on the subject and to promote an understanding of both the issues involved and ways of dealing with them in the context of the Bank's work and of the local conditions in which the Bank operates.[44]

The adviser's position came under the operations policy area, that is, under the functional rather than operational departments of the World Bank. The office was within the Projects Policy Department, which included advisers on project policy, technical cooperation, procurement, public enterprises, public sector management, consultant services, and environmental issues. The WID adviser and her office were not in the project flow because women in development, as a concept, is not considered a sector akin to agricultural and rural development, education, or transportation. Many of the staff members I interviewed had very little interaction with the WID adviser. The office's resources, during Gloria Scott's tenure, consisted of a half-time secretary and a half-time assistant as well as some funds to hire consultants for special studies.

The first WID adviser was succeeded in 1985 by a population economist who had previously been with the Population, Health, and Nutrition Department of the Bank. The Bank's 1987 reorganization brought an upgrading in the adviser's position to that of division chief within the new Population and Human Resources Department under the PPR complex. The WID division now has six professional staff members, though the regional departments have no WID specialists who are directly responsible for integrating WID concerns into Bank projects.

Three WID workshops for Bank staff were held by Scott, taking as their point of departure the premise that women in most developing countries are at a disadvantage when traditional social systems are disrupted by development projects. The main goals of the workshops were to identify the productive activities of women in different contexts and to examine ways of integrating these activities into Bank projects more systematically through better project design, implementation, and monitoring.[45] The participants in workshops included a combination of country program, projects, and operations policy staff, but did not include higher-level staff (division chief and above).[46]

The EDI of the World Bank is involved in the training of developing country personnel. Although the EDI offers no specific WID courses or modules, women's role has been included in courses and discussions related to agriculture and population, health, and nutrition. The International Center for Research on Women prepared an annotated bibliography for EDI to be used in courses and case studies and as a resource for Third World organizations. The EDI's task force on WID issues plans to cooperate with the ILO and the United Nations International Research and Training Institute for the Advancement of Women (INSTRAW) to summarize the experience gained to date. After the reorganization of the Bank, the task force was asked to make strategy proposals for raising gender issues in the EDI's activities. The task force's consensus is to work by integrating throughout the EDI courses and seminars rather than by having separate courses or separate sessions in courses and seminars.[47] For example, a module on rural road maintenance, which is part of a course on transport policy for six sub-Saharan states, has included WID issues.[48] Another study examines the impact of structural adjustment on women's labor in seven countries; and seminars for policymakers on such topics as macroeconomics and communications have included women's issues.[49]

Summary

The extent of the response to WID issues in the Bank, though limited, has increased over time. Specific sector guidelines do not yet exist except in two sectors, and WID issues are not considered at every stage of the project cycle. The WID division does not send its staff on identification missions on a regular basis, and there are no WID specialists in operational departments.[50] There is, however, some evidence that WID issues recently have been considered more extensively in project appraisal reports. The sectors that have the highest level of inclusion of WID issues are population, health and nutrition; agriculture and rural development; and education. Country programs have included women more extensively as a result of President Conable's request.

One of the most significant changes has been the setting up of a Division for Women in Development with six professional staff members. This has made WID issues more visible throughout the Bank, but has a drawback: The WID office is within the PPR, but there are no corresponding WID specialists in operational departments; thus, research, policy papers, and guidelines produced by the WID division may not necessarily be reflected in operational work.

Explanations of the World Bank's Responses

Structural Factors

The development assistance regime and the World Bank. The relevant actors in the Bank's environment, who are also participants in the development assistance regime, include the member governments (both in donor and recipient categories) and other multilateral, bilateral, and nongovernmental development agencies with whom the Bank cooperates. Much of the demand for integrating women into development activities, as we have seen, was initiated within the UN system as a result of the global women's movement. Specifically, specialized agencies within the UN system were invited to achieve the objectives and targets of the UN Decade for Women.[51]

As norms and rules on how to integrate women into development activities began to be formulated under UN auspices, the World Bank, along with other development agencies, began to be sensitized to WID issues. Of course, the UN system cannot actually enforce compliance. Even though the World Bank is a specialized UN agency, it maintains its operations independently and does not report to the UN on its activities as do other specialized agencies. Two of the major reasons for the Bank's independence are that it supplements its lendable funds by borrowing in world financial markets and that it is the biggest provider of both money and technical help to the Third World, with lending operations of $16–18 billion annually. UN activities do influence Bank operations somewhat, however, because the Bank has joint projects with many UN agencies, and their approaches to development issues are bound to have an effect. The fact that the first WID adviser in the World Bank held the position of senior adviser, UN Center for Social Development and Humanitarian Affairs, may demonstrate the Bank's desire to promote good relations with the rest of the UN system. In fact, Bank staff members have attended UN conferences on women and submitted reports on the Bank's progress to the United Nations.

The World Bank is also accountable to the US government because the United States provides a quarter of its capital subscriptions, and the Bank's president has always been a US national. It is likely that US policy on women in development in the early 1970s encouraged the Bank to establish the position of WID adviser.[52] The Bank was one of the international agencies that the 1973 New Directions amendments of the 1972 Foreign Assistance act were aimed at.[53] The Percy amendment supplemented this legislation by calling for integration of women into national economies.[54] The Congress mandated the USAID to implement the Percy amendment and to encourage other donors to give specific attention to women in development.[55] Some Bank staff members believed that the appointment of the Bank's first WID adviser was prompted by USAID and congressional influence. However, interviews also showed that the Congress has not requested any serious follow-up on women in development, other than the short periodic reports to the Congress produced by the Bank's Public Relations Department.

Among bilateral donors, those known to be sympathetic to WID issues—Norway, Sweden, the Netherlands, Germany, and Canada—have provided the leadership in integrating WID concerns into the development assistance regime. In projects they have cofinanced with the World Bank, they have tended to fund a WID component and have encouraged the Bank to consider WID issues. For example, the Bank's work in family planning, nutrition, and health in South Asia includes income-generating projects such as mothers' centers (in which women learn weaving, garment-making, etc.), vocational training schools for women, or women's cooperatives; these activities were financed by Canada. Because these funds are grants, not loans, the Bank lets donors decide what they want to fund. The WID strategy paper on Indonesia (which the Bank prepared at the request of the Netherlands, chair of the donor consortium for Indonesia) and the PROWWESS project are another two instances of the involvement of gender-sensitive bilateral donors in Bank activities.[56]

How have borrower governments influenced World Bank policy on women in development? After the preparation and appraisal of a project comes the negotiation stage, during which the Bank and the borrower attempt to agree on the measures necessary to assure the success of the project. The Bank may conceivably propose conditions in the loan agreements regarding women in development; some respondents did mention this possibility, but also questioned whether the Bank would be interested in using its influence in this area. Others, including President Conable, argued that the Bank can only suggest certain issues to borrower governments—that ultimately they must bear responsibility for attention to women in development.[57]

Borrower governments' interest in and commitment to women in development were mentioned repeatedly as important determinants of its consideration, although it is hard to know whether this argument is being used as an excuse for inaction. The Bank management takes the position that without government commitment, only lip service can be paid to WID policy:

> The legislative, policy and program decisions to improve opportunities for women rest with government. But by paying increasing attention to women's needs in project design and by analyzing women in development issues, the World Bank is helping to create a more favorable climate to improve women's options. If concern for women is to be given more than lip service, it is essential that women's role be considered seriously in policy discussions with development agencies, that women and their organizations take part in such dialogues and that they obtain information about their results, as well as information about development programs and projects about to be financed.[58]

Interviews revealed that many staff members felt the Bank would respond to WID concerns if they were suggested by borrowers, but the Bank was not prepared to push the issue by any such means as making it a condition of loan agreements. Even those who thought that the Bank should make WID components a condition of loan agreements were not sure "how that would go if the Bank started running a crusade." Many thought that countries evolve at their own pace: the Bank cannot force change; it can only promote WID issues, but final decisions rest with the borrower governments. This view, however, may be changing. The Bank has called on Pakistan to reduce discrimination against women, and according to *The Economist*, it also wants the government to put more money into girls' education and women's health: "The Bank reckons that, if more women had paid jobs, parents would be encouraged to invest in their daughters' education."[59]

In cases in which a staff member does make women in development a condition of the loan agreement, the problem of borrower government interest and commitment remains. Because the Bank has relatively little leverage over implementation, it is possible for governments to agree and then bypass the issue. For example, one staff member who worked on an irrigation project for Kenya reported that the Bank had tried to provide funds for women by making a WID component a condition of the loan agreement; since project officers are not involved in implementation, she does not know if the Kenyan government followed through with it or found a loophole allowing it to ignore the stipulation.[60]

Host country governments generally do not see consideration of women as a project design issue. Some staff members mentioned that government attitudes are cynical and that representatives laugh when WID concerns are mentioned. For example, one staff member who worked in a forestry project in India asked that the borrower government set a target that 30 percent of extension workers should be women, but the people just nodded their heads and went about their business—forestry is still seen as a man's preserve. Another staff member on a different Indian project said that host country officials denigrate women: "When you inquire about women, they say, 'You don't want to talk to women, they don't know anything.'" When this person saw there were no women extension agents for women's work, she asked officials about it, but they became defensive. In another case in Malaysia, where she was doing an evaluation study, she found that women did 60 percent of the tapping of rubber trees but got no extension advice; men received the proceeds. This staff member was instrumental in conducting a farm survey and getting data to show the reality of the situation. This particular instance also illustrates the importance of having gender-sensitive members on project, mission, or evaluation teams.

Resistance seems to come especially from those borrower governments whose societies are patriarchal and strongly discriminate against women. By contrast, in countries where women are already economically and politically active, governments seem to display a more positive attitude, and the Bank is more likely to consider women in its country economic reports where they are already prominent. One staff member mentioned that in his experience, it was much harder to consider women in a report on Pakistan than in one on Nigeria or The Gambia, both of whose country reports included women. Examples of successful projects that specifically included women came from countries such as Malawi, Kenya, and Sri Lanka and from the Tamil Nadu state in India, where women are economically and politically active. A Tamil Nadu nutrition and health project for mothers and children is entirely women-driven, with project workers being women. This has been possible because Tamil Nadu recognizes women, there are high-level authorities who are women, and government encouragement made it possible for women to organize cooperatives and run their own project. By comparison, a family planning project in Bangladesh is run by men because of the nature of a more patriarchal society and government attitudes.[61]

The possibility of giving consideration to women in development is increased a great deal if the Bank is the executing agency for a particular project and if the funding agency is interested in WID integration. For

example, some projects in Sri Lanka, funded by the International Fund
for Agricultural Development (IFAD) and executed by the Bank, have
special women's components such as an income-generating plan that
provides small loans to rural industries. The WID component was incorporated because the Sri Lankan government showed interest; a specialized women's bureau was involved; the funding agency was interested;
the project officer was sympathetic; and his division chief showed interest
by asking his staff to include women in development in the Sri Lanka
country programming paper and sectors analysis. Another project funded by IFAD in Yemen included a WID component in its design and a
WID consultant on the project team. As the mission leader explained,
the women's component deals with agricultural extension and is
designed to fill a gap in reaching female beneficiaries and improving
production, was needed because many farmer households are headed by
women as a result of the migration of men, and male extension agents
have not reached female farmers. This project, too, included a women's
component as a result of tripartite interest in women in development.

The Bank also executes a UNDP program titled Development and
Implementation of Low-Cost Sanitation Investment Projects, which takes
into consideration how social analysis can be incorporated into other
types of project analyses. The Technology Advisory Group established
under this project has published a number of papers that deal with how
social concerns, women's interests, and community participation can be
part of water supply and sanitation projects.[62] These and other papers
published by the Urban Development and Water Supply Department of
the Bank contain material, advice, and software for technicians and engineers that are written in a language they know. The objective of this work
is to make sure technicians reach the community, including the women.

These illustrations show that when donors who are also the leaders
in WID issues (such as Northern European donor governments, gender-
sensitive development agencies such as IFAD, UNICEF, or ILO, and
women's organizations in recipient countries) are involved in Bank activities, the chances for the consideration of WID issues increase. The more
visible women's economic activities are and the better organized they are,
the more likely that donors and recipients of aid will include women. For
example, women's concerns came to the agenda in the UNDP water project because Norway, Canada, and the Netherlands funded a project to
incorporate women into water supply and sanitation projects; African
governments involved in the project showed interest; women are clearly
the major project participants and beneficiaries; and there were Bank
staff members who indicated interest in WID issues.[63]

The World Bank's goals and procedures. The World Bank is set up as a bank
and a development institution. As a banking institution, its goal is to

increase its profitability through its lending operations; as a development institution, its principal goal is to increase economic productivity and stimulate economic growth in developing countries. Although this may sound neutral, this goal rests on a neoliberal value system. The principal objective of neoliberalism is economic growth, and the principal routes to growth are seen to lie in capital accumulation and export expansion.[64] The commonly suggested solution is to allow free reign to economics in the form of market forces; that is, the prescription is "market liberalization."[65] In the 1970s, there was heightened emphasis on questions of poverty and income distribution, but this did not mean that the prevalent concern—growth—could be forgotten.

How do gender issues fit into this value system? Interviews revealed that the staff felt justified in concerning itself with WID issues if they serve the goal of economic growth. When economic viability is involved—that is, when the consideration of women is linked to economic productivity and returns on investment—then there is a need to be concerned with the roles of women. This is in line with the dominant ideology, widely shared throughout the Bank, that emphasizes the tenets of neoclassical economics. Concern with women has also been justified as necessary to achieve a decline in birth rates. Rapid population growth acts as a brake on development: Within most countries, for any given amount of resources, a slower rate of population growth would help to promote economic and social development.[66] The goal is to educate women in order to reduce fertility: As women become better educated, health and nutrition practices improve; infant morbidity and mortality decline; marriage and childbirth are delayed; birth rates fall; and preferences for smaller families emerge, with women being more receptive to family planning.[67] Women's economic activity is considered mainly in this context, and income-generating projects are designed for women so that they will have fewer children.[68] For example, population and family planning projects in Bangladesh offer women vocational training and employment opportunities as well as improved health care and family planning services. They seek to raise women's socioeconomic status, thus making them less dependent on the labor of their children and more receptive to the idea of limiting the size of their family.[69] In general, the idea of the instrumentality of women to the goal of economic growth has prevailed—in other words, when gender issues and technical control overlap, the chances for consideration of gender issues increase.

In addition to being considered in the context of economic growth goals, WID issues have also been discussed by development theorists and practitioners within the context of achieving more equitable development. In other words, WID issues are justified as a strategy to empower a section of the population to whom fewer resources have been allocated, or at least to make sure that women are not further disadvantaged. This has been a strictly secondary concern among the Bank staff, in part because questions of equity, social welfare, and distribution do not constitute a priority. Equity issues, even during Robert McNamara's presidency when they were stressed, have not received the same welcome from all staff members; they are not easily quantifiable and they introduce many unknowns. Ascher's research on the World Bank supports this view:

> Many professionals in the World Bank have been reluctant to incorporate new considerations in formulating development strategies if they require modes of analysis less rigorous than the traditional economic framework. . . . Unless and until development strategies can be converted into decision-making procedures acceptable to the professional norms of those entrusted with using them, the implementation of these strategies is bound to meet resistance.[70]

Many staff members pointed out that if it were economically viable, the Bank would consider women—but not because they are women. Most of the staff was unwilling to discuss the role of women as a fairness/equity issue and did not see increasing women's status or women's empowerment as relevant to their work. This reaction is despite the fact that the Bank has been on the forefront of development thought in the 1970s on poverty-oriented development and basic-needs strategies that could encompass the idea that a more equitable development should include women. Although many staff members are interested in problems of social justice, welfare, and equity, they are uncomfortable with these issues. There is no good theory on equity and economic productivity and the link between the two: Many economists see efficiency and productivity as value-neutral, equity as value-laden and subjective.

The consideration of women separately on the basis of their differential access to resources implies that they may be disadvantaged and that this imbalance may need to be corrected for reasons of social justice and equity. This is nothing less than asking for the empowerment of women, but such empowerment brings with it a whole host of uncontrollable factors in the environment. It shifts attention from the design/planning phase of project organization where control may be exercised to the implementation and evaluation phase where the Bank has to deal with client participation. But the intended beneficiaries may request a project entirely different from the one proposed by staff, or the borrower government may be unaccepting of the increased political awareness and voice that accompany empowerment. The Bank is not ready to push for such a goal, whether it is the empowerment of women or the empowerment of project beneficiaries as a whole. It is unwilling directly to attack the social structures of a society.

There is, however, much less resistance to increasing women's status indirectly if it maximizes developmental investments and decreases population growth. If, for example, women's status increased as a result of an income-creating project for women, and the income-generating component is the means to decreased fertility, then it is considered justifiable. Education for women is seen in the same context: Education may empower women, but the justification for educating women is decreased population growth in the long run.

Consistency of procedures with WID. The Bank's expertise in economic and technical analyses and the training of its staff to conduct these analyses constitute the means—the technology—to achieve the Bank's ends. The Bank's procedures focus on the calculation of economic or financial rates of return, and the analyses required must be technically rigorous, expressed by quantitative measures of inputs delivered and returns on investment. In contrast, social analysis, within which WID policy issues have usually been placed, and institutional analysis are relative latecomers that are not as well accepted and integrated into the Bank staff's work because they are less determinate, require some experimentation, and therefore are not compatible with technically rigorous analysis.

Interviews with Bank staff members, including those who wanted to integrate WID issues into their work, revealed the widespread feeling that the work done in the past to raise consciousness and increase sensitivity to women now had to be replaced with "operationalization"—integrating the issue into the Bank's project analysis. The WID adviser has suggested following available social techniques in order to make WID issues more operational. At the identification stage of a project (which includes its design, preparation, and appraisal), a social assessment study can be done that ranges from extensive primary data-gathering activities to rapid field analysis of existing data over a two- to three-week period. Such data may be organized into categories: women's social and economic activities; women's access to and control of resources; and benefits to women. The second step after the collection of data is a feasibility analysis, which would assess whether assumptions about project populations and their response are likely to be borne out in practice during implementation. In the case of gender issues, this step would consist of asking some key questions on how to increase women's productivity, access to and control of resources, and project benefits and how to eliminate any negative effects of the project on these factors. Possible questions might include these: Have women's needs been assessed? Do project objectives reflect these needs? Have women participated in setting these objectives? Have the project's impacts, positive and negative, on women's activities been identified? Are project implementation and evaluation geared toward women's needs, toward delivering goods and services to women beneficiaries?[71]

The next step is the applied use of social information or the incorporation of special components into the design in order to ensure that target groups or others will cooperate with or benefit from the project, or that the project's unintended negative consequences will be minimized. Finally, forecasting social impact and measuring project impact would identify the groups that would be affected, or adversely, whether positively and in what ways.

How do these techniques and procedures fit into technical and economic analysis? One World Bank study indicates the following problems:

> Social inputs and specialist services have been most frequently used in the past for social assessment {background data collection usually} and for measurement of the impact of a project—activities that are both data intensive and fairly high in cost. They are therefore difficult to incorporate routinely into Bank project work in all sectors requiring only some attention to users' questions and are sometimes too cumbersome to serve the needs of busy decision-makers. Available techniques are not particularly well adapted to the operational needs and time constraints of the project cycle. They are largely perceived as descriptive data included in appraisal reports because they are required.[72]

This study also points out that the major reason for resistance to social analysis is the difficulties encountered in the applied use of social information and analysis during the design stage of a project: "While the theoretical basis of social feasibility is well-developed, its application to development planning and project issues is less advanced."[73]

Besides the emphasis on technical, economic, and financial analyses, the emphasis on the timely delivery of the project through the pipeline has important implications for the consideration of gender issues. Bank staff members are required to get a certain number of projects approved by the Board of Executive Directors in a given amount of time; in other words, the Bank's output is defined in terms of timely delivery. As Judith Tendler's study on the USAID has shown, the way organizational outputs get defined in terms of quantitative measures—of moving large amounts of money, or of returns on investment—exerts an overriding influence on project organization.[74] Such a definition of output acts as a disincentive to the consideration of women.

Many staff members emphasized the negative consequences of having to define output in terms of timely delivery. The effect on the Bank's staff is a continuous feeling of being rushed and meeting tight deadlines, which results in the avoidance of complex issues that would take extra time, would need experimentation, or would expose a lack of knowledge on the part of the staff. WID issues are new on the agenda and require experimenting with pilot projects, but there is little time for that because projects in the pipeline have to be approved quickly. Consideration of gender issues would slow the project approval process and increase complexity and uncertainty in the work of the staff.

Many staff members mentioned that the Bank's scale of lending puts a constraint on the consideration of women. Women are usually involved in small-scale activities, but the Bank's loans are large for cost-effectiveness reasons. It was also mentioned that because the Bank's primary focus is on financial considerations, it tends not to be flexible or experimental, both conditions that would help the integration of women into the Bank's activities. The Bank's own evaluation of its performance reflects awareness of these issues:

> Both Mr. McNamara's Nairobi address to the Board of Governors in September 1973 and related reports and policy statements proclaimed an increased Bank emphasis on agricultural lending and on channelling it more directly towards the poor. That strategy recognized the need for innovation and experimentation and the greater associated risks of such lending. Despite the call for experimentation, Bank staff did not bring forth in adequate numbers the types of high-risk, but low-exposure pilot projects that, with hindsight, the circumstances demanded. The demands on staff time for such work was hardly less than that for more conventionally sized projects, and the pressures of pre-ordained, rapidly expanding lending programs and of additional concerns for the environment, the role of women, and other emerging issues simply meant that much of the experimentation that took place intruded into conventionally sized projects.[75]

The problem of demands on staff time was echoed in interviews; many complained that tight deadlines leave absolutely no time to consider all the issues. This was especially true for project staff: "I try to include women in development issues in my work, but especially after I have joined the projects department, it has become much harder to do so because there are so many requirements set by management in project work that the staff is already overworked and spread thin. Women in development may be considered only if there is time."[76] Under these constraints, WID issues receive only ad hoc consideration:

> The project officer is like a jack-of-all-trades, but with so many things to do, he or she pays attention to social analysis selectively. Including women in development depends on the initiative and interest of the individual project officer. Time is limited and project officers, once they go to the field, have to take responsibility for things that are not their specialty, which means perspectives are short-run and they sacri-

fice certain things. Limitations on time and money and the necessity to prioritize issues means they have to make major compromises.[77]

The emphasis on feeding the project pipeline encourages front-end planning. Thus, the emphasis is on project design, preparation, and appraisal rather than implementation and evaluation. The staff is rewarded for appraisals and negotiations regarding projects, and promotional prospects depend in large part on a staff member's ability to process projects quickly and smoothly. At the same time, there is no penalty for those who are responsible for projects that founder:

> Project completion work gets shortchanged. Staff is not held accountable if project outcomes are bad—for example, for not considering women properly—but they get "brownie points" for creative analysis at the project design and appraisal level. There is no accountability for projects that fail except in multicomponent projects. When it is the same type of project that fails over and over again, then lessons get fed back and projects evolve.[78]

Ironically, the rationale for WID policy is based on implementation problems by showing, ex post facto, that lack of attention to women's activities and to women's access and control of resources causes project implementation to fail or suffer. There are many examples of this: Under a project in the Bolivian Altiplano, where women have responsiblity for livestock, training in husbandry was nevertheless given to the men, who passed the information to their wives with inevitable and costly omissions. Efforts in several countries to introduce improved stoves under Bank-assisted projects have been unsuccessful; although the stoves used fuel efficiently, they did not satisfy women's requirements.[79] But because project organization does not allow for adequate supervision and there is little accountability for failed projects, showing that lack of consideration of women contributed to the failure of a project creates little impact. Furthermore, even making such a showing is not the same as proving what precise elements should have been incorporated into the project cycle in the first place. Criticisms about lack of attention to women might create resentment among staff instead of serving as constructive criticism; resentment causes staff members to see WID issues as constraints—as something extra among the many other factors they are asked to consider without being given adequate time or resources.

In short, technically trained staff members show considerable resistance to what is perceived as soft data that produce murky conclusions: They are usually not trained to conduct social analysis and generally have a low regard for it; they perceive it as adding to uncertainty, leading them to an area in which they have to admit a lack of knowledge and forcing them to compromise the technically rigorous analysis they are trained to conduct. This makes the incorporation of women into project analysis difficult.

Another constraint on incorporating WID concerns is the operation of the checks-and-balances system between regional offices (including project and program departments) and the operations policy offices that deal with sectors. As pointed out earlier, before the reorganization of the Bank, the WID adviser was not in the project flow and could only present criticisms of projects already designed, effectively halting their progress. An assistant to the WID adviser mentioned that she was reticent about making too many criticisms, knowing that the project staff was already overworked and that she might sound as if she were "policing" it. The new Division for Women in Development is structurally more powerful, but still suffers from this system of organizational accountability that divides responsibility for projects between operational staff and PPR staff. Operational staff at times resents the advice given to it by the functional units, claiming that these staff members sit behind desks dispensing advice while operational staff members are in the field struggling with reality. Interviews revealed that papers produced by the WID division may not necessarily be read by operational staff and that the influence of functional departments has declined as a result of the restructuring. The upshot is that one cannot assume the research carried out by the PPR complex is being integrated into the operational work of the Bank.

Choice Factors: The Internal Bargaining Process

Even though organizational conditions shape performance, there is still room for a range of strategies WID policy advocates can use to persuade the professional staff of the relevance of WID issues to their work as well as to elicit the support of the management. It is important that such advocates understand the constraints that arise from organizational goals and procedures. Some staff members felt the first WID adviser did not form networks with other Bank staff supportive of WID issues; rather than working inside the Bank to prepare the ground for a more influential advocacy office, she focused her efforts toward justifying the Bank's work to the outside. Many staff members, even those who had done WID-related work, mentioned they had very little or no contact with the WID office. They felt the WID adviser was effective in representing the Bank on WID issues to the outside, though some staff members suggested more can be achieved inside the Bank by attending project design meetings and talking to relevant projects staff than by attending women's conferences. Staff generally perceived her post as a political or public relations position; many viewed it as a political, consciousness-raising job.

Before she retired in 1985, Scott confirmed the perception that her main achievement had been defending the Bank to the outside:

> I think perhaps one of the things I have taken some satisfaction from is how much [what] I have been doing in the Bank is regarded as providing intellectual leadership in other agencies, little though it is. For instance, when I wrote the "Invisible Woman" in 1979, I thought it was just a little progress report for the Bank. But it became guidance material for other multilateral, bilateral and nongovernmental agencies because the material was specific and raised operational issues which had not been dealt with before.[80]

Scott has said that in spite of her goodwill efforts, she did at times doubt the management's commitment to WID policy: "And although I've had to constantly defend the Bank as being really serious about these issues, it became increasingly difficult to do so over the years. Why? Because I myself doubted the Bank's commitment."[81]

The Bank's management has not encouraged a meaningful response to women in development until very recently. WID policy has been articulated in speeches and general policy statements by top management (the president and vice-presidents), but there is widespread consensus among the staff that had management taken seriously the incorporation of women into the Bank's development activities, the treatment given WID issues in terms of the Bank's organizational structure would have been very different. In other words, the authority structure would have changed to accommodate gender issues: "Management does not see this as an important issue that serious professionals have to consider; there is no serious mandate. It is never mentioned in regular management seminars. Among management, one's generation and individual orientation determine interest in women in development issues."[82]

Many of the staff members said that because the WID adviser had only a part-time secretary and a part-time assistant, she could not realistically be effective in such a vast institution as the World Bank. The fact that resources are so meager was seen as an indication that WID is paid only lip service—in fact, some saw the presence of the adviser as a diversionary tactic that let the management avoid having to do anything substantial about women's problems in development processes. Scott also was not in a good position to convince the professional staff of the importance of WID issues. She was not a Bank staff member with technical expertise and was seen as an affirmative action case. Her origins, the Commission of Humanitarian Affairs of the United Nations, reinforced the suspicion that the Bank was merely responding to outside pressure but had no real intention of including women in development in its "technical core."[83] In fact, the establishment of the WID adviser's post may, as James Thompson has suggested, be a case of an organization acting to protect its technical core from sources of uncertainty in its environment: By establishing what he calls "boundary spanning mechanisms," such as advocacy offices, organizations respond to threats in the environment, co-opt political energy, and seal off those offices from their technical core.[84]

The current chief of the Division for Women in Development has taken care to make WID issues acceptable by framing them within economic rather than social welfare and equity arguments. Herz's strategies have been to promote the legitimacy of WID concerns among the Bank staff and to foster close ties with the management. She has the credentials and expertise to help WID issues become a more serious, more legitimate topic among the staff, and because the Bank has primarily been interested in women as part of the population-related issue, her training in population economics gives her credibility. She has been instrumental in organizing a conference on safe motherhood; she has outlined a new WID policy that focuses on specific sectors and geographical areas and that aims to make WID issues part of country policy dialogues;[85] and she has started going on project identification missions, thus getting the chance to provide input at an early stage of projects.

Barber Conable, who became the World Bank president in 1987, has indicated strong interest and commitment to WID issues:

> Regarding population, the environment, and the role of women, we should work on all three fronts at once. It is clear that population pressures are one source of heavy environmental damage, so we must provide training to give women the skills to take charge of their productive and reproductive lives. And it makes little sense to fund agricultural extension services and credit programmes in Africa that do not reach the real farmers, the women who work the land.[86]

Other members of the management have also expressed concern about WID issues. For example, the vice-president for Eastern and Southern Africa asked his staff members to include WID objectives in their work programs, and the Bank's senior vice-president for operations asked the WID adviser to explore the idea of country strategies with the regional offices and other donors and to report back to him with a possible approach and a list of countries from which to select. Interviews revealed that even though senior management was enthusiastic about WID issues, mid-level management's attitude was at best "benevolent tolerance" and at worst "hostility." This attitude can best be explained by the constraints posed by the organizational goals and procedures of the Bank.

Conclusion

The incorporation of WID issues into World Bank operations has been increasing, and the leadership of the Bank's gender-sensitive partners has played an important role in introducing WID issues as part of the development assistance regime. The increased attention to WID issues at the international level, especially since the 1985 Nairobi conference, has had an effect on the World Bank. Several actors acting in concert make consideration of WID issues by the Bank more likely: when the borrower government is interested; when the Bank is the executing agency for a project and the funding agency is interested; and when the particular Bank staff involved is interested. In short, when various actors in a position to influence Bank policy simultaneously demonstrate sensitivity to WID issues, attention to WID tends to increase.

Because the norms and rules of the development assistance regime are filtered through organizational factors, the extent to which the Bank incorporates women in development into its activities depends on the consistency of WID goals with the Bank's goals and procedures, as well as on the bargaining power of the internal WID advocates. As one staff member put it, women are not ignored on purpose. However, they are not intentionally included either. The conclusion is that WID issues have been treated as residual matters that may or may not be addressed depending on the interest of the staff and the management and the time allocated to each operation. What has been done has not been done as a matter of Bank policy but of personal inclination. As another staff member put it: "The Bank has not yet seen the need to address women and development issues in a systematic way and has not taken the initiative to experiment with it. There is no real commitment to increase women's status through projects." This resistance is explained by the limited fit of WID issues into the Bank's goals and procedures.

The recent progress can be explained both by the increased acceptance of WID policy by the Bank's partners within the development assistance regime, and by the efforts of staff members who have acted as WID policy entrepreneurs in the WID division as well as in operational departments. WID issues have received a more favorable response from staff members when they were introduced and justified on the basis of economic viability. The more the indispensability of WID components to the economic success of projects can be demonstrated, the more staff members are likely to pay attention. Over time, the number and quality of such demonstrations have increased, as has the legitimacy of WID issues. Still, for more extensive incorporation of WID issues in the World Bank, a critical number of middle-level managers and project officers will need to be convinced that considering WID issues will improve the economic

viability of projects, and this will need to be accompanied by more extensive acceptance of the integral role of WID issues within the development
assistance regime.

Notes

1. World Bank, *The World Bank Annual Report 1985* (Washington, DC:
World Bank, 1985), p. 3.
2. World Bank, *Questions and Answers: The World Bank and IDA*
(Washington, DC: World Bank, January 1974), p. 3.
3. Ibid., p. 5.
4. Ibid., p. 10.
5. Ascher, "New Development Approaches."
6. Robert Ayres, *Banking on the Poor* (Cambridge: Massachusetts Institute
of Technology Press, 1984), p. 66.
7. World Bank, *The World Bank Annual Report 1989* (Washington, DC:
World Bank, 1989).
8. The following discussion draws from Ayres, *Banking on the Poor.*
9. Warren Baum and Stokes M. Tolbert, *Investing in Development: Lessons
of World Bank Experience* (Washington, DC: World Bank, 1985), pp. 337–355.
10. World Bank, *Annual Report 1989,* p. 59.
11. Augusta Molnar and Gotz Schreiber, *Women and Forestry: Operational
Issues,* Policy, Planning and Research Working Paper, WPS 184 (Washington,
DC: World Bank, May 1989).
12. World Bank interviews, Washington, DC, May 1986.
13. These projects do not constitute a scientific sample of all projects that
include WID factors.
14. At time of publication of this book, a comprehensive report detailing
the activities of the Division for Women in Development was being prepared for
presentation to the Board of Governors but had not yet been made public. Like
the UNDP sample, the World Bank sample is meant only as an illustration.
15. World Bank, *Agricultural Research and Extension: Evaluation of the World
Bank's Experience* (Washington, DC: World Bank, 1985), p. 84.
16. World Bank, *Tenth Annual Review of Project Performance Audit Results*
(Washington, DC: World Bank, 1985), pp. v, 49.
17. World Bank, *1985 Annual Review of Project Performance Audit Results*
(Washington, DC: World Bank, 1986), pp. 17, 68.
18. World Bank, Operations Evaluation Department, *Cotton Development
Programs in Burkina Faso, Cote d'Ivoire and Togo* (Washington, DC: World Bank,
1988), pp. x–xi.
19. This assessment was made on the basis of an examination of staff
reports, staff working papers and policy papers, and interview responses.
20. See World Bank, *Abstract of Current Studies: The World Bank Research
Program* (Washington, DC: World Bank, 1978); *Abstract of Current Studies: The
World Bank Research Program* (Washington, DC: World Bank, 1984).

21. UN, *Newsletter on the Status of Women* (June 1974): 12.

22. World Bank, *World Development Report 1984* (Washington, DC: Oxford University Press, 1984), pp. 106–126.

23. World Bank, *World Development Report 1984*, pp. 109–110.

24. See, e.g., David Wheeler, "Female Education, Family Planning, Income, and Population: A Long-run Econometric Simulation Model," in *Three Cross-Country Analyses of the Effects of Organized Family Planning*, ed. Nancy Birdsall (Washington, DC: World Bank, 1984).

25. World Bank, *World Development Report 1984*, pp. 110–111.

26. Ayse Kudat and Helen Abadzi, *Women's Presence in Arab Higher Education: Linking School, Labor Markets and Social Roles*, Working Paper (Washington, DC: EDI/World Bank, 1989).

27. Interview with Barbara Herz, "Mothers: Ultimate Resource," *Development Forum* 15, 3 (April 1987): 3 and 12.

28. Ann Starrs, *Preventing the Tragedy of Maternal Deaths—Report on the International Safe Motherhood Conference, Nairobi, Kenya, February 1987* (Washington, DC: World Bank, 1987); Barbara Herz and Anthony R. Measham, *Safe Motherhood Initiative: Proposals for Action*, World Bank Discussion Paper No. 9 (Washington, DC: World Bank, 1987).

29. P. H. Coombs with M. Ahmed, *Attacking Rural Poverty: How Nonformal Education Can Help* (Baltimore and London: Johns Hopkins University Press, 1974), cited in World Bank, *Rural Development*, Sector Policy Paper, February 1975.

30. Gloria Scott and Marilyn Carr, *The Impact of Technology Choice on Rural Women in Bangladesh: Problems and Opportunities*, Staff Working Paper 731 (Washington, DC: World Bank, 1985); Meena Acharya and Lynn Bennett, *Women in the Subsistence Sector: Economic Participation and Household Decision-Making in Nepal*, Staff Working Paper 526 (Washington, DC: World Bank, 1983).

31. World Bank, Office of the Adviser on Women in Development, "Forestry Projects and Women," unpublished paper, September 1980.

32. Barbara Herz, "The World Bank Proposed Work Program for Women in Development," internal memorandum, December 6, 1985.

33. World Bank, "Women and Development in the Water Supply and Sanitation Sector in Latin America," internal memorandum, October 1985.

34. Ibid., pp. 3–4.

35. UNDP, "Girl Guides Inspire Health in Thailand's Poor Northeast," *Source* (December 1989): 16.

36. UNDP, *Women in Development: Project Achievement Reports from the UNDP,* June 1988, p. 36.

37. World Bank, Technology Advisory Group, *Involving Women in Sanitation Project Planning and Implementation* (Washington, DC: World Bank, 1985).

38. See, e.g., John Briscoe and David de Ferranti, *Water for Rural Communities: Helping People to Help Themselves* (Washington, DC: World Bank, 1987).

39. Two examples are by Ayse Kudat, *Women's Participation in Human Settlements Management* and *Communications, Women and Settlements Management,*

Working Papers (Washington, DC: EDI/World Bank, 1988.

40. Rakesh Mohan, *Labor Force Participation in a Developing Metropolis: Does Sex Matter?* Staff Working Paper 749 (Washington, DC: World Bank, 1985); Nwanganga Shields, *Women in the Urban Labor Markets in Africa: The Case of Tanzania,* Staff Working Paper 380 (Washington, DC: World Bank, 1980).

41. Herz, "Proposed Work Program for Women in Development."

42. World Bank, "Indonesian Women and Development," unpublished paper, April 30, 1985.

43. Herz, World Bank internal memorandum, April 10, 1986.

44. World Bank, *Annual Report 1984,* p. 68.

45. World Bank, internal memorandum, January 27, 1983.

46. Ibid., p. 2.

47. Personal correspondence with a staff member, May 1987.

48. Ayse Kudat, *Women's Participation in Rural Road Maintenance in Sub-Saharan Africa,* Working Paper (Washington, DC: EDI/World Bank, 1988).

49. See, e.g., Kudat, *Communications, Women and Settlements Management* and *Women's Participation in Human Settlements Management.*

50. In June 1990, a WID specialist in the Environmental Unit of the Technical Department, Asia Regional Office, started work.

51. United Nations, International Women's Year Secretariat, *Meeting in Mexico: World Conference of the International Women's Year 1975* (New York: Center for Economic and Social Information, 1975).

52. See Tinker, "Women in Development."

53. US Congress, House of Representatives, *Foreign Assistance Act,* 93d Cong. 2d Sess., PL 93-189, 17 December 1973, Sections 103–107.

54. Ibid., Section 113.

55. US Department of State, Agency for International Development, "Integration of Women into National Economies," Policy Determination 60, 16 September 1974.

56. UNDP, *Source* (December 1989): 16.

57. Barber Conable, televised panel discussion on World Food Day, 6 October 1986.

58. World Bank, "The U.N. Decade for Women," *The Bank's World* 4, 9 (September 1985): 12.

59. *The Economist* (13 January 1990): 38.

60. World Bank interviews, Washington, DC, May 1986.

61. These examples were cited in World Bank interviews, Washington, DC, April 1986.

62. See, for example, World Bank, Technology Advisory Group, *Involving Women in Sanitation Projects.*

63. Staff at both the World Bank and the UNDP indicated that some Bank staff members working on water supply and sanitation projects had a gender-sensitive approach. It was mentioned in interviews that staff members working in the Africa regional office have a similar attitude.

64. See Ayres, *Banking on the Poor,* pp. 74–75.

65. See, e.g., Michael Bratton, "The Comrades and the Countryside: The Politics of Agricultural Policy in Zimbabwe," *World Politics* 39, 2 (January 1987):

174–202.

66. See World Bank, *World Development Report 1984,* which focuses on population change and development.

67. Baum and Tolbert, *Investing in Development: Lessons of World Bank Experience,* p. 484.

68. World Bank interviews, Washington, DC, April 1986.

69. Baum and Tolbert, *Investing in Development,* p. 489.

70. Ascher, "New Development Approaches."

71. World Bank, Office of the Adviser on Women in Development, "A Framework for Analysis," unpublished paper prepared for the Workshop for Women in Development, 19–21 January 1983.

72. Francis Lethem and Heli Perrett, *Human Factors in Project Work,* Staff Working Paper 397 (Washington, DC: World Bank, June 1980), p. 7.

73. Ibid.

74. Tendler, *Inside Foreign Aid.*

75. World Bank, *1985 Annual Review of Project Performance Results,* p. 38.

76. World Bank interviews, Washington, DC, May 1986.

77. Ibid.

78. Ibid.

79. Baum and Tolbert, *Investing in Development,* pp. 484–491.

80. World Bank, "Q and A with Gloria Scott," *The Bank's World* 4, 9 (September 1985): 6.

81. Ibid.

82. World bank interviews, Washington, DC, May 1986.

83. James D. Thompson, *Organizations in Action* (New York: McGraw-Hill, 1967).

84. Ibid., pp. 21, 39, 50.

85. Herz, "Proposed Work Program for Women in Development."

86. "World Bank Poverty Pledge," *Development Forum* 15, 1 (January-February 1987): 12.

4

Egalitarianism and the Ford Foundation

The Ford Foundation's response to WID issues has been very different from that of the World Bank or the UNDP. The Foundation is a private, nonprofit institution established in 1936 by Henry and Edsel Ford in Michigan. It made grants largely to that state's charitable and educational institutions until 1950, when it began to address national and international problems. According to its self-definition, the Foundation "seeks to identify and contribute to the solution of problems of national and international importance." The Foundation "grants funds to institutions and organizations for experimental, demonstration and developmental efforts that promise to produce significant advances in various fields."[1] Including fiscal year 1987, the Foundation has made commitments totaling $6.6 billion, the recipients of which have been located in the United States and various foreign countries, especially in the Third World. Approximately 35 percent of the Foundation's budget is allocated for work in developing countries. This constitutes roughly $2.3 billion of total commitments.[2]

Foundation policy is determined by a Board of Trustees, made up of leaders in business and academia. This board names the president of the Foundation, and it is at the level of the Board of Trustees that broad problem definition occurs. Although the self-replacing board has rights of discretion and disposal over the resources of the organization, it does not deal with specific grants but instead approves the allocation of resources to broad programming areas. The president directs the implementation of policy determined by the board and approves most grants; the vice-presidents and representatives in field offices have the authority to approve grants up to $50,000. A professional staff evaluates grant applications, works with prospective grantees, and recommends proposals for approval by the president and the trustees.

Until 1982, the Foundation was divided into three divisions, each with its vice-president: education and public policy; national affairs; and international affairs. The International Division had six New York–based subdivisions: vice-president's office; European and international affairs; population; Asia and the Pacific; Middle East and Africa; and Latin America and the Caribbean. The three latter subdivisions, known as area offices, each had a head, located in New York with a back-up staff of program officers, and there were field offices throughout the developing world, each headed by a representative and usually backed up by program officers and program advisers.

After 1982, the Foundation was restructured into two program divisions, each with its vice-president: US and international affairs programs; and developing country programs. The thematic program areas are the same for both divisions and are identified as urban poverty; rural poverty and resources; human rights and governance; education and culture; and international affairs. The Foundation has thirteen field offices around the world located in Dakar, Lagos, Nairobi, Cairo, Dhaka, New Delhi, Jakarta, Beijing, Lima, Rio de Janeiro, Mexico City, Manila, and Bangkok. The total number of professional staff as of 31 December 1987 was 177; 54 percent were women and 17 percent were minorities.[3]

Response to WID Issues

Policy and Procedures

President McGeorge Bundy created a Foundation-wide task force on the status of women in 1972, which marked the International Division's official recognition of women as a separate programmatic concern. As one observer of the Foundation remarked, women were not taken seriously by the men who consider themselves at the fore of development issues.[4] Along with the establishment of this task force, the International Division's vice-president, David Bell, named the division's representative on the task force, Elinor Barber, to chair a committee on women's programs. This committee was assigned the task of reviewing periodically the progress made in women's programs and suggesting changes in Foundation strategy. Bell, in an internal memorandum, made a powerful statement of the leadership's recognition that WID issues were legitimate. He pointed out that program efforts had previously been confined to improving the lives of women in their traditional roles; he called on the field offices to go beyond that and to initiate "a serious effort to examine the role of women and to consider the complex questions of equal opportunities, social justice, and personal fulfillment which are so rightly of such deep concern to so many women in the world."[5]

In 1974, special money for promoting women's projects in the form of a Delegated Authority Project was approved. The Foundation viewed the 1970s as an exploratory phase in women's programming:

In this exploratory period [1970s], field office grant making often proceeded on an ad hoc basis as the staff tested a variety of approaches and as groups came forward with specific proposals. Staff members, however, were identifying needs and appropriate strategies to address them. Where feminist organizations were relatively strong, grants helped further their efforts. Where they were not, the Foundation provided resources for women to speak and publish and encouraged the incorporation of women's issues into existing organizations. By 1979, International Division spending on women's programs had totaled some $5.2 million and showed promise for continued expansion.[6]

In 1980, with the board's approval, special general reserve funds totaling $19.3 million were allocated to women's programming in both the United States and developing countries.[7] This signified a major expansion in the Foundation's activities concerning women. Beginning in April 1980, $8.7 million from the general reserve was allocated to women's programming for an eighteen-month period. These funds were to be used for staffing, program development, and grant and project action. The special appropriation aimed to integrate concern for women's issues into every relevant area of Foundation work both in the United States and overseas. The eighteen-month increase for the International Division was $4.25 million, with 80 percent of the increase from the general reserve fund. The budgeting process approved by the trustees for the special appropriation contained a built-in funding incentive. It offered a four-to-one match for regular budget funds redirected to support women's grants, spurring staff members to make an effort to increase grants related to women.

Another procedural change was an external affirmative action policy requiring that applications for grants include tabular presentation and interpretation of data on the gender of boards and staff of all grantees, and that grant letters express the Foundation's concern that the grantee give appropriate attention to providing opportunities to women.[8]

Programs

The Foundation's approach, on the whole, has been that women's programming requires both projects targeted directly at women and the integration of women into regular grants and projects. The trend over time has been toward more integration and mainstreaming activities. The Foundation has made many grants that include activities related to women, such as in education, training, income generation and employment, and institution building. For example, grantees such as the Grameen Bank, which provides credit for landless people in rural

Bangladesh, reach large numbers of women as well as men.[9] There are, however, difficulties involved in measuring the extent of women's programming when it is mainstreamed, and such an assessment, to my knowledge, has not yet been undertaken because its effects are harder to discern and document than are those of grants directly aimed at women. I therefore provide data for women-specific grants and confine my discussion of mainstreaming activities to illustrative examples.

Overall, the Ford Foundation made 378 grants related specifically to women in developing countries between 1972 and 1988.[10] An analysis of these grants and Foundation documents indicates that programming for women can be divided into two distinct time periods: 1972–1979 and 1980–1988. These periods differ significantly from each other in terms of both the number of grants and thematic emphases.

During the period 1972–1979, the emphasis was on research on women's roles in society, and on support for the university education and professional training of women to enable them to assume leadership positions in public life. For example, in the area of education, support was provided to Kenya to evaluate leadership training programs for women; to Airlie Foundation for travel costs of participants in the Women's International Forum on Population and Development; to Carlos Chagas Foundation for a program of research on the work and education of women; to Coordination of Initiatives for Development in Latin America for a documentation center on women's roles in Latin American society; to Wellesley College for a conference on women and development; and to the University of Dar es Salaam for graduate fellowships for women students. In the area of agricultural development, a number of grants in Bangladesh supported research and publications on rural women's activities; Foundation funds went to the Integrated Rural Development Programme (a Bangladesh government agency) to establish a pilot project to organize women into rural cooperatives.

During this period, institutional support went to research centers and universities to set up or strengthen women's studies and studies related to women's economic activities. For example, with Foundation support, Beirut University College established in 1973 the Institute for Women's Studies in the Arab World. Other organizations that received Foundation assistance include the ATRCW, to conduct research and provide training to women, and the Jamaica Women's Bureau, to set up a program of services to rural women. Individual female scholars also received grants. A few grants focused on women's legal rights issues; the Bangladesh Institute of Law and International Affairs received funding for a research project on women's legal status in the country. In the area of health and family, the Foundation made grants that directly related women's roles to family planning. The Colombian Association for the Study of Population, for example, received a grant for a study of how childbearing decisions of Colombian women are affected by such variables as employment, education, health, legal rights, and the position of women in the family and society.

Out of 378 grants related to women in 1972–1988, only 52 (14 percent) were allocated between 1972 and 1979. The breakdown of these grants by subject area is shown in Table 4.1; education received the most grants (27), legal rights the fewest (3).

Table 4.1 Ford Foundation Women-Specific Grants by Subject Area, 1972–1988

	1972–1979	1980–1988[a]
Agricultural Development	9	118
Education	27	133
Institutional Support	5	31
Legal Rights	3	17
Health, Family, and Nutrition	8	27
Total Projects	52	326

Source: Information made available by the Ford Foundation.
[a] To March 1988.

The subject areas in Table 4.1 do not directly correspond to the program areas of the Ford Foundation; they were chosen to facilitate comparison with the UNDP and the World Bank. As I define these categories, the area of agricultural development encompasses rural women's economic activities both on and off the farm, including grants for research, training, and action related to agriculture and rural development. The education category includes grants made to support formal educational activities, research on women's roles in society, seminars, conferences, and publications. Institutional support is defined as either core support or support to start up a new program or institution related to women's activities. The category of legal rights refers to activities in women's political, economic, and social rights and their advocacy. Health, family, and nutrition includes support for research in these areas, as well as support for programs and institutions that train, educate, or treat women in areas of reproductive health, nutritional status, and children's health.

The period 1980–1988 brought both a significant increase in the number of grants related to women and a shift in focus. The thematic emphasis changed from grants for research to grants for productive activities of poor rural women; grants related to rural women's economic activities jumped from nine to 118. These grants focused on enhancing the productive capacity of low-income women through skills training, cooperative organization, production and marketing, and introduction of improved technologies.[11] Support went to several countries: A pilot project for village-level women agricultural extension workers was undertaken by the government of Karnataka in India. Tamil Nadu Agricultural University received funds for a pilot project to train selected village women in the development of small sericulture and dairy farms. The International Reconstruction Fund of Nicaragua received support to examine the role of women in Nicaraguan agricultural cooperatives. The University of Abadan got support for experimental village women's income-generating projects in Oyo State, Nigeria. The Association for the Advancement of Economic and Social Knowledge got technical assistance for income-generating projects for women in central Java. Such grants encouraged rural development organizations and agricultural universities to include both women and women's concerns in their staffing, planning, and extension work. Other grants addressed women's off-farm work, such as those made to test a number of small-scale projects including soap-making, market gardening, and goat-raising. Aid went to an experimental revolving loan fund for rural women producers in Mali. In India, grants were made to upgrade skills and economic return in silk production and dairying, which employ large numbers of women.

Grants in family and health areas concentrated on rural women's health and the training of alternative health workers. For example, the Bangladesh Women's Health Coalition was supported for an experimental rural women's health care project. The International Women's Information and Communication Service received support for a Latin American and Caribbean Women's Health Network; and the Self-Employed Women's Association in India received Foundation support to establish community-based health care. Again in India, the Andhra Pradesh Dairy Development Cooperative received funds to integrate child survival and women's health services into a cooperative dairying program.

In the area of legal rights, the Nepal Women's Organization got support for strengthening and expanding its legal services project. The Pontifical Catholic University of São Paulo was funded for a popular education project on women's rights and political participation, and the Overseas Education Fund received support for a planning meeting and Asia-wide conference of the Women, Law and Development Forum. The Amman Business and Professional Women's Club obtained a grant for a legal aid and counseling service for low-income urban women in Jordan, and the Institute for Consultation and Legal Aid for Women and Families was given support for the development of legal aid clinics in seven provincial cities of Indonesia.

The Foundation has continued funding research to incorporate WID issues into curricula both in US universities and policy centers and in Third World universities and research institutes. Examples of the latter are grants made to the Women in Development Unit of the University of the West Indies, to the African Association of Women for Research and Development in Senegal, and to the Development Studies Research Center of the University of Khartoum.

In summary, the number of women-related grants in the period 1980–1988 has increased substantially; these accounted for 86 percent of the total number of grants between 1972 and 1988. Thematic focus in the early period was support of research and its dissemination and of formal education related to women and women's roles in society; the emphasis shifted in the 1980s to rural women's economic activities, legal rights and advocacy, and women's reproductive health. The total amount of funds allocated to grants related to women in developing countries between 1972 and March 1988 was approximately $27.5 million.[12] Of this amount, about $5.1 million was allocated between 1972 and 1979, the rest between 1980 and 1988.

Staffing

Beginning in 1976, one-and-a-half positions were funded under the Delegated Authority Project in the International Division in New York to provide assistance to field offices in instituting women's programming. The full-time position was that of a "circuit-riding" program officer—based in the headquarters but making extensive trips to field offices to proffer advice and help in developing women-specific grants. When women staff members were hired, their responsibilities included exploring program possibilities related to women.

In 1980, using the special appropriations for women's programming from the general reserve, the trustees funded a full-time officer in charge of Foundation-wide women's programs. To oversee the expanding grant program, the Foundation created the Women's Program Group (WPG) made up of program staff. The WPG's mandate was to increase awareness of sex discrimination and to propose solutions by inviting guest speakers, holding seminars on various topics, and sending relevant publications to field offices. This group functioned as a cross-program consulting and review committee and reported regularly to the president and the trustees. After the special appropriations period ended, the WPG was replaced by the Women's Program Forum, which received an internal grant of $160,000 to monitor progress in women's programming, maintain visibility of women's issues, and stimulate other donors in this area. The name of this forum was later changed to the Working Group on

Women, and this group was included in all grant-making considerations; its chair reported to the president and the Board of Trustees. In many field offices, the Foundation added new staff members who focused on women's issues or assigned a staff member to be responsible for women's issues.

A significant indicator of the Foundation's commitment to women's programs is the appointment of two WPG members known to be strong advocates of women's issues to key positions in the Foundation. When the Foundation was reorganized in 1981, Susan Berresford, who had headed various Foundation-wide committees on women, was named vice-president for US-based programs. Another major WID advocate, Adrienne Germain, who had served as the circuit-riding officer for women's programs, was appointed as Foundation representative in Bangladesh. Both appointments marked the first time women were named to such high posts.

Table 4.2 Percentage of Women Among Ford Foundation Personnel

	1973	1979	1986
Trustees	12.5	15.0	17.6
Professional Staff	22.9	32.6	53.2
Support Staff	89.1	86.2	86.0

Source: Adapted from *Created Equal* (New York: Ford Foundation, October 1986), p. 14.

The Ford Foundation also has focused on changing female-to-male staff ratios. Although there is no direct correspondence between the number of women and attention to women's issues in an organization, if a significant percentage of professional staff is women, then the likelihood of attention to women's issues increases. By 1986, women accounted for 53.2 percent of professional staff (see Table 4.2); they made gains of 20.6 percentage points in representation on professional staff between 1979 and 1986. The infusion of new, mostly female staff members and the creation of the circuit-rider position, according to a 1986 Foundation report, brought "new perspectives, new energy, and increased numbers of staff members who constituted a support group as needed."[13] Sensitivity to gender issues was considered an important criterion for job candidates, a situation that prompted them to consider gender issues. New women staff members, particularly those hired in New York, were able to add a development rationale for the inclusion of WID programs and were able to continue pressure for those programs.[14] As the Foundation's staff began to search out groups that women had formed or that worked on behalf of women's interests, this search was facilitated—particularly in countries in which segregation of the sexes in public life is the rule—by the increasing presence of women on the Foundation's program staff.

Explanations of the Ford Foundation's Response

Structural Factors

The development assistance regime and the Ford Foundation. I have argued in previous chapters that the rise of an international women's movement and the gradual increase in the legitimacy of WID issues affected the response of development agencies. In the case of the Ford Foundation, the Foundation itself has provided leadership for placing WID issues on the international agenda. The Foundation's interest in women's issues, both in the United States and the Third World, and its support of academic research and development projects directed at women have established it firmly as a major supporter and promoter of WID issues within the development assistance regime.

Women's concerns were initially recognized by the women's movement in the United States and the rest of the Western world. Similarly, in the Foundation, the initial impetus to recognize women's concerns came from the division responsible for national affairs, which was already making grants for women's programming in the early 1970s. Feminists were part of the professional personnel within both national and international divisions. As an observer of the Foundation pointed out, the exchange of ideas between division staffs, especially after the organizational restructuring in 1981, has played a significant role in the success of women's programming in developing countries.[15]

The Foundation's support for research on women has been instrumental in the building of a knowledge base on women's issues in development. Without this knowledge base, the development assistance regime cannot be changed. As universities start integrating WID issues into their curricula, as research and policy institutes start publishing documents on WID concerns, and as policy activists begin pressing national governments and international organizations, WID issues gain visibility and legitimacy. Policymakers and development planners whose education exposed them to WID issues are more likely to be responsive than are those for whom WID concerns are a nonissue.

A good example of the ripple effect of Foundation support for research on women is the international conference at Wellesley College in 1976 on women in development; selections from this conference were later published in a 1977 issue of Signs and as a book,[16] and the conference has been hailed as one of the major gatherings that helped establish women in development as an academic field.[17] The Foundation's support for research has not only focused on establishing the legitimacy of women's issues in development, but has also helped to encourage dialogue among researchers, policymakers, and donors. For example, in May 1988, the Foundation sponsored a cross-regional symposium in Nairobi, Kenya, on income-earning opportunities for poor women; it was attended by major donors, recipients, and NGOs. The goals of this symposium were to focus the donor community's attention on women; to encourage the allocation of more overall funding for women; and to discuss strategies of assistance in the area of employment generation both in general and specifically for women.

The Ford Foundation's role within the development assistance regime is particularly well-suited to provide leadership in new issues. With a staff of just 177 professionals, the Foundation is relatively small, both in terms of personnel and resources, especially compared with other international development agencies: Its commitments through 1987 totaled $6.6 billion, as compared, for example, with the World Bank's $16–18 billion annually. Organization theorists suggest that small bureaus tend to be more flexible and innovative than large ones.[18] Given that women's organizations are generally small, that their capacity to absorb large grants is limited, and that some of their activities are new and untried, the relative smallness of Foundation grants makes it possible to set up pilot projects and test new approaches. And given that the Foundation sees itself in a position to voice the concerns and interests of groups hitherto excluded from the benefits of society, it is clear why WID issues could be received favorably.

Another aspect of the Foundation's role within the development assistance regime is that it sees itself as a mediator among nongovernmental groups, governments, and other donor agencies. It is in a unique position among donor agencies in that it deals with all involved. As one staff member stated: "The Foundation offices function as a conduit, as a catalyst to build links between the governments, NGOs, and other donor agencies."[19] So, too, does the development literature discuss the role of the Foundation as a catalyst that can help achieve policy reforms. Policy reforms require complex institutional changes in a local context, and performance in this arena depends on the exercise of creative initiative by many individuals.

Both political leaders and the large donors commonly find their sources of leverage to be of relatively little consequence in achieving policy objectives. As an example of what he calls "a micro-policy reform," Korten cites "agricultural extension projects [that] can demand that the research-extension system be responsive to farmer realities and inputs. But if the existing structures are geared to enforcing farmer compliance with centrally mandated technology packages and there is no tradition of researchers seeking feedback from extension agents, such responsiveness is unlikely until these structures are transformed."[20] Korten provides an example of how the Ford Foundation served as an effective catalyst to bring about policy reform in Southeast Asia by promoting, through its regional office, community-based approaches to resource management in its work in irrigation and social forestry. The strategy included two key elements: (1) the formation of a coalition of individuals committed to change who bring with them the resources of a number of relevant institutions and form a working group and (2) the assumption of leadership by this working group in documenting and analyzing available experience, planning pilot activities, and initiating a variety of actions leading to the institutionalization of policies and supporting capacities within the agency:

> The Ford Foundation program officers serve as facilitators of the process, identify prospective working group members, support their involvement in relevant activities, and help them establish distinctive roles within the working group. At the same time they play a key role in agenda-setting. . . . Flexible funding is provided in the form of grants to the sponsoring agency for related experimental and research activities. . . . Occasionally the Ford Foundation program officer will develop his or her own study illuminating key program and policy issues input to working group sponsored workshops.[21]

The linkages the Foundation has built with other actors of the development assistance regime and the nature of its role in building and supporting these linkages have important implications for women's programming. For example, as a staff member explained, when Foundation-sponsored workshops were held and case studies carried out on women and their activities in the irrigation sector in the Philippines, the manuals of the Philippine National Irrigation Authority were rewritten to include women.[22]

The area of women's programming was identified by the Foundation as a niche in which its initiative and leadership would be valuable:

> These proposed program directions [production and income generation, training, and women's rights and advocacy] complement the work of other agencies. Many governments and most large international agencies, such as USAID or the World Bank, have an expressed interest in women's roles in development and, in most cases, one or more staff assigned to develop programs. To date, however, it is fair to say that these agencies, for the most part, have either been ill-suited for or uninterested in the kinds of activities outlined above. Nonetheless, we have effectively collaborated with other donors and hope to continue and expand that collaboration.[23]

More recently, a 1986 report on women's programs emphasized the importance of the Foundation's role as a conduit between such organizations and governments and other development agencies:

> For several field offices, future employment and income-generation projects will have two principal aims: increasing the scale and sophistication of such projects, and the direct benefits for poor women; and increasing their influence on development policies and policy makers. . . . The Foundation will also encourage attempts to ascertain policy implications of women-specific projects and to present these findings to decision makers, planners and public and private development organizations. Despite progress in the past decade, most development agencies still undervalue gender differentiation in planning and carrying out their activities. In both the United States and developing countries, the Foundation will encourage affirmative action to bring women knowledgeable about employment and income-generation projects into "mainstream" development agencies and community revitalization. And because the Foundation is in many places uniquely positioned to facilitate contacts between women's groups and other development organizations, the staff will encourage such collaboration.[24]

The Foundation has reinforced this leadership role by its publications on women. Policy statements for the future and reports on past activities related to women were published, such as *That 51%, That 51% Plus, Women in the World,* and *Created Equal.* Forty-five thousand copies of each have been distributed; as a result, donors and prospective grantees became aware of the Foundation's interest and commitment to women's issues.

In short, WID issues are new, experimental, and require research; women's organizations are usually small and require smaller grants. The Foundation has unique advantages to deal with WID issues and act as a leader in incorporating them into development theory and practice.

Goals and procedures. The Ford Foundation's self-described goal is to find solutions to problems of national and international importance through experimentation in education, science, and the arts. Its organizational structure, procedures, and staff reflect this goal, which in turn has influenced the nature of women's programming in particular ways.

The Foundation staff believes that conditions in the Third World are best explained by inequitable allocation of resources and the lack of voice for the poor and powerless. In the Foundation's vision, the good society is pluralistic, diverse, equitable, and nondiscriminatory. This value system provides bases for action and understanding because suggestions for action are based upon it. A value system also binds together its adherents. The management of an organization can, by encouraging certain values, develop stronger goal consensus among staff members. Management can also use these values in selective recruiting to attract potential members who will contribute to stronger goal consensus, and to repel those with adverse goals. In the Ford Foundation's case, recruits generally share the goals articulated by the Ford Foundation's values, in part because they may already share these values and in part because of the training and orientation they receive after they are hired. Staff members have a reputation for being progressive and committed to social issues. They generally have a background in academia, public policy, research, law, or government organizations; and they are trained to analyze and act upon social, political, economic, and legal rather than technical issues. One should not underestimate, however, the extent of goal consensus that can develop after joining an organization. As one staff member stated: "All staff members have social and communication skills, but they are not necessarily naturally oriented to equity and empowerment issues. In the latter case, the management orientation is important. After they come, they get trained to consider them."[25]

How has this value system influenced the approach to gender issues? Strategies are called for that will help the disadvantaged and the poor—that will build their capacity to participate in society on an equal basis. Concern for women fits into these strategies easily because feminism is defined in the Foundation literature as "a concern for redressing unequal power based on gender."[26] A variety of activities around the world to improve women's status and opportunities become worthy of consideration based on concern for social justice.

Several procedures of the Foundation have been helpful to consideration of women. First, when the Foundation enters a new area, it makes grants for basic research, applied research, and action programs, in that order. "As staff members have learned, research in a new field is often a first step toward more direct 'hands-on' approaches that incorporate research findings into their design. The results of these approaches then feed back into further documentation and research, which in turn leads to further action."[27] The Foundation's practice of funding research has been an advantage for women's programs. The production of knowledge on women's roles and experience in society and its dissemination constitute the first steps toward action. As a new field, gender issues in development needed data and information before women could be integrated into development programs and projects in the Third World. The Foundation's activities related to funding research by and on women have helped to identify program areas that need action.

Second, the procedures also emphasize close interaction between program officers and the management. The Foundation has some of the same traditions of colleagueship present in university situations.[28] Access to managers is relatively easy, and they are known to be receptive to new ideas: "Staff members' ideas are accepted and encouraged by management. . . . If you have an idea or a problem, you can talk to the person directly above you or you can go to the vice-president, and it is perfectly acceptable to do the latter."[29] For the WID policy advocates within the Foundation, this easy access has been to their advantage because they have had the opportunity to make new proposals.

Third, the Ford Foundation combines aspects of centralized and decentralized decisionmaking. Although the headquarters is responsible for making general policy and for hiring all staff, the field offices have a great deal of decisionmaking power in grant making. They allocate 90 percent of the developing country grants for international and regional programs. Field offices are authorized to make grants up to $50,000 independently; for larger grants, approval may take the form of advice rather than full-scale revisions or refusals. As one staff member indicated: "The representative in the field decides what grants should be approved. The negotiation takes place between program officers and the representative regarding a grant decision. Officially every grant has to be approved centrally, but headquarters may just review and offer suggestions."[30] Thus, the implication for women's programming of this structure is that field offices have the freedom to encourage and respond to proposals made by women's organizations, as well as to take the initiative in seeking them out.

Choice Factors: The Internal Bargaining Process

Goals and procedures may encourage the consideration of a new issue, but without internal advocates, there is no guarantee that it will be considered seriously. The Ford Foundation has had a group of staff members who chose to commit themselves to advance WID issues in Foundation activities and were instrumental in bringing about change.

The initial impetus for change in women's programming included efforts for affirmative action within the Foundation as well as efforts to win equal rights and opportunity for women in the United States and elsewhere. In 1970, a staff committee recommended the following changes within the Foundation: adoption of an affirmative action program to increase the number of minority and women professionals on the staff; appointment of women to the Board of Trustees; adjustment of pay differentials between male and female professionals; and broadening of maternity and child care benefits. Within the Foundation, the "women's question" became a matter for debate in late 1971, with the preparation of the discussion paper "Planning for the Foundation

Program in 1973 and Beyond." This planning document treated women as a separate topic and was approved by the Board of Trustees in March 1972.

As with the international movement to recognize women's concerns, the impetus within the Foundation came from its "First World"—the divisions of national affairs, education, and research in the headquarters. The activist roots of feminists who were part of the professional staff in these divisions led them to organize to pressure internally for change. Many staff members mentioned the high level of commitment and interest on the part of those staff members who became the policy advocates on behalf of women's issues, and the centrality of their commitment to the response of the Foundation to gender concerns. It must be mentioned that these staff members were not all women; of the eighteen WPG staff members, for example, six were men.

Consensus-building activities. A major goal of the WID advocates was to build consensus on the significance of WID issues for the Foundation's development work. Even though women's issues clearly fit into the Foundation's focus on equality, staff members have not automatically seen the importance of women to development efforts. The information papers written by WID policy entrepreneurs, which provided a rationale for WID issues, and their networking efforts have been instrumental in consensus building. In 1974, Germain joined the Office of Population, leading to the modification of program priorities to include a formal commitment to research and action on the status of women, with emphasis on how status relates to fertility behavior. This focus lent a new rationale to women's programming, based not on social justice—women's status must be considered because it is right to do so—but on development—women's status must be considered because effective and egalitarian development cannot occur without changes to increase women's participation in the total process.[31]

The International Division's staff initially saw gender concerns as a social justice issue spurred by the feminist movement in the United States rather than as a development issue. To overcome this resistance, the women's lobby introduced the discourse on women using as its basis the Foundation's interest in overcoming discrimination, but also stressing the importance of increasing productivity and overcoming poverty in developing countries. They argued that improving women's economic roles would achieve the dual objectives of sexual equality and economic betterment. They placed sex discrimination in a global context and justified their protest against it not only as a matter of defending fundamental rights but as a means to invigorate development strategies in the Third World. "Sex discrimination is a universal problem. It exists in varying forms and degrees, but everywhere girls' and women's basic rights, opportunities and development are circumscribed, and societies are deprived of their skills. Sex discrimination is a major factor in poverty and a costly constraint on productivity. It pervades all institutions with strong reinforcement from culture and custom. Wherever and however it exists, it is unjust."[32]

The WPG, which was formed in 1980 after the approval of a special appropriation for women's programs, planned activities that encouraged attention to women's issues in the Foundation programs. For example, all staff members were invited to a series of discussions and films on feminist issues, and mailings on US, European, and Third World women's affairs were sent out every month to overseas representatives and to office heads in New York. This information included papers, memoranda, newspaper articles, reports, and books recommended by group members or requested by staff.[33]

WID advocates have not restricted their interest to internal matters. They have also been involved in networking activities that have contributed to the rise of the international women's movement. The UN International Women's Year (IWY), for example, provided a symbol around which such networks could be built. Women on the Foundation staff sought work with the IWY effort, defining four areas in which the Foundation could play a role: (1) data collection; (2) supporting women who wish to organize to formulate an agenda for government action; (3) sponsorship of conferences; and (4) day care for children.[34] The WPG (and its successor groups) in the Foundation sponsored seminars and symposiums that involved the donor community and expanded the network of actors interested in WID issues. An example is a September 1986 symposium to address the changing context for women's issues; another is the previously mentioned meeting held to discuss income-earning opportunities for poor women. In fact, the mandate of the Women's Program Forum (which replaced the WPG in 1986) explicitly states: "[The Women's Program Forum was] recently established to provide opportunities for discussing issues related to women's programs within the Foundation, to encourage new and expanded grant making for such programs throughout the donor community, and to work as a catalyst to translate into reality the goals of the United Nations Decade for the Advancement of Women."[35]

Policy-relevant activities. The background papers that laid out new ideas, objectives, and budget levels for future women's programs and led to their expansion in 1980 were written by WID policy entrepreneurs inside the Foundation. The original $8.4 million allocation for 1980–1981 rose to $19.3 million. To oversee this growing grant program, the Foundation created a women's program office in January 1980, chaired by Berresford. Berresford suggested that field offices come up with at least partial funding for women's programs with the balance supplied from general reserves. As one staff member pointed out, the matching-fund mechanism[36] spurred field offices to consider women's programs, and every field office either hired a women's program officer or required greater attention to women by all program officers.

The WPG began meeting with the authors of all Foundation information papers (which are the basis for program planning) to ensure women's inclusion as a major part of national and international efforts. The WPG was charged to undertake two types of work:

1. For the women-specific grant program:
   - Consult with experts inside and outside the Foundation to refine program strategy and evaluation;
   - Identify opportunities for cross-divisional collaboration in planning, operating and evaluating programs;
   - Facilitate program development in response to trustees' suggestions that attention be given to long-term implications of changing sex roles; and
   - Oversee spending under the special appropriation and establish a system for Foundation-wide reporting on the women's program.

2. For other Foundation grant programs and administrative matters:
   - Review the Foundation's programs and administrative activities to identify women's issues where they may have been given insufficient attention.[37]

WPG activities included review of Foundation programs not specifically directed at women as well as practices and policies of special importance to women. The WPG was instrumental in putting the Foundation's external affirmative action program in place. Furthermore, the WPG held interviews with candidates for employment in order to acquaint them with the expanding women's program, and the group chair interviewed most final candidates for professional staff positions, not just those concerned specifically with the women's program.[38]

The efforts of WID policy entrepreneurs received strong support from President Franklin Thomas. Advocates of new issues within an agency need allies in management who can provide the resources and the incentives required for the incorporation of new policy. The management's role is especially important in the Ford Foundation because it serves as a mediator between the staff and the Board of Trustees; the latter makes the decisions regarding the broad allocation of the Foundation's resources. The management presents proposals for new programs to the board only when it has a reasonable expectation that the board will look upon the proposals favorably or at least be willing to discuss them. This makes the role of the organization's leader crucial in promoting or blocking new initiatives: "Ideas are not developed extensively unless the board of trustees is going to approve them. The staff deals with the management. The management determines whether the new proposals should be presented to the board and sounds out the board before actual presentation of a proposal is made."[39] In the case of women's programming, the WID advocates found support from senior management. When the Board of Trustees met in 1980, one of the proposals recommended by President Thomas was an increase in the allocation of funds to programs for women. The information paper presented to the board for the December 1979 meeting is introduced by a memorandum from President Thomas in which he declares:

> In my view we gain perspective on an important sector of the Foundation's work through the comprehensive approach of this paper [written by staff members]. The paper recommends continuing some of our present women's programs, starting some new efforts within each division, and allocating additional funds for these purposes in FY 1980 and FY 1981. . . . With the benefit of the Board's general views, I propose to consider this area of our work for additional funding from the General Reserve in both the present budget year and the next.[40]

Staff members indicated in interviews that the president was personally committed to women's programming. Flora, who wrote on the Foundation, also commented that "for many in the field, despite an eight-year push to include women, the president's personal insistence on explanations for women's absence in program development inspired creative inclusion of women."[41] As some staff members observed: "There is no question in anyone's mind that this is something that the management wants us to pay attention to."[42] The endorsement by the board and President Thomas and the seriousness with which they approached program expansion contributed significantly to the success of women's programming. Foundation staff members quickly learned of the subject's importance, their obligations to be informed about it, and recognition for success in programming. Thus, the question was not whether to fund programs in support of women but how to do so most effectively.[43]

Conclusion

Without the efforts of staff members who acted as WID policy entrepreneurs and the strong support they elicited from senior management, WID issues would probably have remained dormant in the Foundation. Instead, as a result of the consensus-building and policy-relevant activities of committed staff members, the Foundation became a leader in WID issues and has played a central role in integrating these issues into the norms and rules of the development assistance regime. WID policy advocates succeeded in achieving significant budget allocations for women's programming and in effecting procedural and staffing changes that helped to integrate women's issues into the Foundation's work. It must be remembered that their choice to engage in internal bargaining was accompanied by favorable structural factors.

The Ford Foundation has unique advantages within the development assistance regime that enable it to act as a leader in new, untried approaches to development. As a private, voluntary organization, it is freer to take initiatives. In fact, the Foundation's self-perception as an innovator and a pacesetter encourages it to redefine issues and in general act as an advocate for social change. The Foundation's goal of finding innovative solutions to social problems encourages experimentation and an active search for new ideas; this goal in turn rests on a value system that emphasizes equity of social groups. The positive response of the Foundation to an emerging international women's movement that demanded nondiscrimination seems natural given its organizational characteristics. As Ruth Leeds has shown in her analysis, organizations with abstract normative goals, such as the Ford Foundation, are more responsive to social movements that attempt to redefine or broaden these goals.[44]

Notes

1. Ford Foundation, *1987 Annual Report* (New York: Ford Foundation, 1987).

2. Ford Foundation, *Current Interests 1988 and 1989* (New York: Ford Foundation, 1988).

3. These statistics were made available to me by the Ford Foundation, New York, in March 1988.

4. Cornelia Butler Flora, "Incorporating Women into International Development Programs: The Political Phenomenology of a Private Foundation," *Women & Politics* 2, 4 (Winter 1982): 93.

5. Ibid., p. 94.

6. A Delegated Authority Project in this case provides Foundation staff

with flexible funds to make small, individual and institutional grants for program development and evaluation. This program was research oriented and worldwide in focus.

7. The general reserve serves as a flexible instrument for meeting unanticipated needs and responding to unusual program opportunities.

8. Ford Foundation, "Interim Report on the Expanded Women's Program," unpublished paper, February 1981, p. 16.

9. Ford Foundation, *Created Equal* (New York: Ford Foundation, October 1986), p. 52.

10. This analysis is mainly based on data furnished by the Ford Foundation Archives of projects between 1975 and 1988 that include the word "women" in the title.

11. This discussion and that in the section headed "Changes in Staffing" draw from Ford Foundation, *Created Equal.*

12. This is an approximate figure calculated from documents made available to me by the Ford Foundation.

13. Ford Foundation, "Women's Programs: Past, Present and Future," unpublished paper, June 1986, p. 50.

14. Flora, "Incorporating Women," p. 104.

15. Conversation with Judith Tendler, East Lansing, MI, March 1988.

16. Wellesley Editorial Committee, ed., *Women and National Development: The Complexities of Change* (Chicago: University of Chicago Press, 1977).

17. Jaquette, "Women and Modernization Theory."

18. Downs, *Inside Bureaucracy*, p. 202.

19. Ford Foundation interviews, New York, March 1988.

20. David Korten, "Third-Generation NGO Strategies: A Key to People-Centered Development," *World Development* 15 (Autumn 1987): 152.

21. Ibid., p. 153.

22. Ford Foundation interviews, New York, March 1988.

23. Ford Foundation, "Programs for Women: Plans and Budgets for Fiscal Years 1980 and 1981," unpublished paper, March 1980, p. 35.

24. Ford Foundation, "Women's Programs: Past, Present and Future," unpublished paper, June 1986, p. 49.

25. Ford Foundation interviews, New York, March 1988.

26. Ford Foundation, *Created Equal*, p. 1.

27. Ibid., p. 23.

28. Flora, "Incorporating Women," p. 90.

29. Ford Foundation interviews, New York, March 1988.

30. Ibid.

31. Flora, "Incorporating Women," p. 96.

32. Ford Foundation, *Women in the World* (New York: Ford Foundation, 1980), p. 3.

33. Ford Foundation, "Interim Report on the Expanded Women's Program."

34. Flora, "Incorporating Women," p. 102.

35. Ford Foundation, "The Changing Context for Movements to Improve Women's Lives: Proceedings of the Ford Foundation's Women's Program

Forum," unpublished paper, 29 September 1986.

36. Ford Foundation, *Created Equal,* p. 30.

37. Ford Foundation, "Interim Report on the Expanded Women's Program."

38. Ibid.

39. Ford Foundation interviews, New York, March 1988.

40. Ford Foundation, "Programs for Women: An Information Paper for the Board of Trustees," unpublished paper, December 1979.

41. Flora, "Incorporating Women," p. 100.

42. Ford Foundation interviews, New York, March 1988.

43. Ford Foundation, "Women's Programs: Past, Present and Future," p. 43.

44. Ruth Leeds, "The Absorption of Protest: A Working Paper," in *New Perspectives in Organizational Research,* eds. W. W. Cooper, H. J. Leavitt, and M. W. Shelly II (New York: Wiley, 1964), pp. 115–135.

5

Bringing Women In

The International Women's Movement and the Development Assistance Regime

Gender issues were put on the agenda of development agencies as a result of the international women's movement that emerged in the early 1970s. Beginning in 1975 at the World Conference of the International Women's Year in Mexico and throughout the UN Decade for Women (1976–1985), members of this movement articulated its goals in governmental and nongovernmental forums.[1] These goals included the alteration of the development assistance regime—an alteration that would involve increased access and resources for women within development programs and projects and the formulation of gender-sensitive policies by governments and international development agencies.

By the end of the Nairobi conference, which marked the conclusion of the UN Decade for Women, there was no question of the success of the international women's movement. The conference adopted guidelines (*The Nairobi Forward-Looking Strategies for the Advancement of Women*) that formulated standards regarding development assistance and stipulated that bilateral and multilateral agencies' policies for women in development should involve all parts of donor organizations and that WID programs and policies should be incorporated into all agency procedures at program, project, and sector levels.

The UN's efforts to change the norms, rules, and procedures of the development assistance regime have been accompanied by a vast array of indigenous women's movements and women's leadership initiatives in Third World countries.[2] Women seek both self-determination and empowerment, but also demand a voice in the social, economic, and political structures controlling their lives. The forms and strategies of the women's movement in the Third World are too numerous to list here, but some examples will illustrate their nature and breadth. Over the past decade, more than a hundred new women's centers have been formed in

Latin America to address women's work, legal issues, health, sexuality, reproductive problems, and participation in national liberation struggles. The Development Alternatives for Women in a New Era is a significant example of a project led by women from the Third World, presenting Third World feminist perspectives on a range of issues but particularly on new strategies to reconceptualize development. Another initiative comes from the Asian Women's Research and Action Network, which organized women from seventeen countries in the region to write alternative reports on the impact of the Decade for Women so that governments would not be the only voice representing women at the 1985 Nairobi conference.

Development agencies have begun mainstreaming women's issues into their activities; donors now consider WID concerns not just in projects but also in their sector and policy-related work.[3] There is, of course, a long way to go before WID issues become an integral part of the development assistance regime, accepted and acted upon by all actors involved. This resistance stems partially from the nature and influence of the women's movement and partially from the nature of the regime. Oran Young has provided some interesting hypotheses to explain international regime formation, which may shed light on the opportunities and constraints the women's movement has faced in altering the development assistance regime. Among the six conditions he cites that make regime formation more successful are if issues can be presented in "contractarian" rather than distributive terms; if salient solutions and clear-cut and effective compliance mechanisms exist; if there are exogenous shocks and crises that contribute to increased efforts to negotiate; and if effective leadership emerges.[4]

How did the international women's movement fare in creating these conditions? The aim of any social movement is to enter the political realm and change the rules of the game in a way that takes the interests of its participants (in this case, the interests of Third World women) into account.[5] However, the very characteristics that help a social movement succeed as a movement may often inhibit it once it enters the political realm. Many concrete, accepted rules of the game exist, and newcomers are expected to abide by them. These rules are manifested in both institutional values and norms of behavior and in policy and procedures. Thus, the policy impact of a social movement depends upon framing demands within existing institutions.

These institutions, of course, by their ability to reward or punish efforts for change with success or defeat, often can reshape social movements; those that conform to norms of behavior in order to participate successfully in political institutions often forsake their major goals for change and become reformist. Thus, the international women's movement, in order to have a policy impact in development agencies, has had to frame its demands in reformist terms—seeking modification of development agencies so that women are better incorporated into existing institutions rather than proposing fundamental changes in established power structures. Bargaining has taken place in contractual rather than distributive terms: The arguments have been that if women are taken into consideration in development, everyone will win; the state of families, societies, and development efforts will all improve. Instead of addressing women in their own terms, the agenda of the Nairobi conference focused on women as a key resource to accomplish the goals of development, showing that these desired ends would be compromised unless attention is paid to women as a key resource. However, when fundamental changes in power relations between men and women are implied, the resistance to WID issues is much greater.

Exogenous shocks, in this case, have been the failures of the UN development decades and the worsening poverty in the Third World. These crises have made it possible for members of the women's movement to frame women's issues as part of the concern for poverty alleviation. Furthermore, effective leadership on behalf of women has been exercised by some members of the development assistance regime, such as Northern European and Canadian bilateral aid agencies, NGOs (e.g., the Ford Foundation and OXFAM America), some UN organizations (e.g., the ILO), and some indigenous women's organizations in the Third World. However, because the regime is composed of many actors (donor agencies and governments, recipient governments, NGOs, and others) and is virtually completely decentralized, overall integration of WID issues into development assistance activities is still to come.

What most effectively constrains the efforts of the international women's movement are the requirements for salient solutions (or focal points describable in simple terms) that increase the probability of success in institutional bargaining, and the need to establish clear-cut and effective compliance mechanisms. The paucity of research and knowledge about women's activities and of methodologies that translate women's issues directly into project and program documents have restrained the response of actors within the development assistance regime. Problems related to compliance with norms, rules, and regulations are, of course, not unique to this field: "The lack of well-entrenched and properly financed supranational organizations in international society ensures that international regimes must rely heavily on the ability and willingness of individual members to elicit compliance with key provisions within their own jurisdictions."[6]

Because the international development assistance regime is weaker and more decentralized than, for example, the monetary or trade regime, it proves that much more difficult to penetrate. Many actors and many viewpoints exist, and international norms and rules clash with those of local jurisdictions. Establishing salient solutions and assuring compliance are rendered still more difficult because any social movement, by its very nature, is unable to devise implementable, concrete rules and regulations. The problems the US women's movement met in influencing the Congress apply to the international women's movement as well:

> The power of social movements to focus diffuse public pressures is tremendous, especially at the agenda-setting stage of the policy process. But the dynamism of a strong social movement may alienate legislators and other top decision-makers. Groups that emerge from movement politics must learn to convert their strength into concrete proposals, actual laws and implemented policy, and many social movements encounter considerable difficulty in changing the thrust of their activism to deal effectively with "nuts and bolts" concerns.[7]

Efforts to alter the development assistance regime at the international level have elicited quite varied responses from individual actors. Regime analysis, which provides useful insights about the formation, activities, and decline of regimes, has paid less attention to how regime norms are translated into policy within specific organizational contexts. This is where organizational analysis can complement regime analysis and expand our understanding of how international organizations respond to changes in regime norms. The World Bank, the UNDP, and the Ford Foundation have responded differently to WID issues. This difference can be explained by the position of each organization in relation to other actors within the development assistance regime and by the goals and procedures of each agency. Furthermore, the success of WID policy entrepreneurs inside these agencies depends upon their ability to show their colleagues that WID issues are consistent with the goals and procedures in each agency and upon their ability to influence policy. Even though these agencies are not a representative sample of all actors within the development assistance regime, the findings imply that as its norms and rules have begun to integrate WID issues, actors within the regime respond in different ways depending on different organizational contexts.

Responses of Three Agencies

The changes in policies, procedures, programming, project activities, and staffing in the three agencies indicate that there is a range of responses, with the UNDP at the low end, the World Bank somewhere in the middle, and the Ford Foundation at the high end.

The UNDP had no concrete WID policy until 1986, after which came establishment of the Division for Women in Development and the development of comprehensive WID guidelines. Mechanisms for the implementation of these guidelines include the participation of the WID division director in the action committee meetings that give final approval for projects over $700,000 and the project review forms and questionnaires on WID-related activities that country offices have been asked to fill out. These forms, the first attempts at systematically monitoring the integration of women into UNDP projects, are expected to serve as a baseline for future monitoring and tripartite reviews.[8]

Since 1984, more specific guidelines have been produced on forestry and agricultural extension and credit by the Division for Women in Development, but there are no specific procedures as such that ensure the inclusion of women in Bank projects. Even though the staff is asked to discuss WID issues in appraisal reports, they are responsible for many other issues as well. Further, appraisal reports do not reflect what actually happened at implementation; it is thus difficult to show any systematic inclusion. The consideration of WID issues depends more on the particular focus of the WID division and on the interest of staff members and management in particular departments. More recently, President Conable has asked staff members to discuss WID issues and how they will integrate them into their next three-year work plans. This may, in fact, encourage a more systematic consideration.

The Ford Foundation went furthest both in setting up specific procedures to facilitate inclusion of WID policy in its activities and in formally involving staff members. Important procedural changes include the four-to-one budget-matching mechanism and flexible funding measures such as those pertaining to Delegated Authority Projects. These provided special money for promoting women's projects, allowing the staff to make small individual and institutional grants for WID program development and evaluation. Another important procedural change was the institution of an external affirmative action policy, which requires that the forms requesting grant action show evidence that grantees are giving appropriate attention to the provision of opportunities to women. Finally, a group of staff members under the name of Women's Program Group (later Women's Program Forum) has had the responsibility to review all grant proposals for WID content, to interview prospective staff members, and to report to the president and the trustees on the progress of women's programming in the Foundation.

The small number of projects with WID content that the UNDP has made public for illustrative purposes does not form the basis for a conclusion about the extent of WID integration in all UNDP activities. However, a comparison of a group of earlier projects with later projects does show that there is a move toward mainstreaming WID activities. There is also indication of more interest in women in development in regional and interregional projects than in specific country projects. A study sponsored by the Division for Women in Development on UNDP country programs discovered that so far there been no systematic integration of WID issues at the level of country programming.

In the World Bank, as in the UNDP, the sample of project appraisal reports with WID content does not allow generalizations about all Bank projects. However, over time, assumptions that women will automatically benefit from a project seem to have been replaced by a trend toward providing women with tools, training, and education within Bank projects. The World Bank's work at the country level has begun to include WID issues: One of the new initiatives of the Bank's WID office is the development of WID country strategies that are intended to influence the advice and loans the Bank provides to developing countries. So far, strategy papers have been written on WID issues for seventeen countries.

The Ford Foundation's WID programming, which dates to the early 1970s, emphasizes Third World women, especially in the areas of research and education. In 1980, special general reserve funds totaling $19.3 million were allocated to women's programming in both the United States and developing countries.[9] Grants for women in developing countries increased from 52 for the period 1972–1979 to 326 for 1980–1988.[10] The focus of these programs also changed: After 1980, more attention was given to women's rural development activities, legal rights and advocacy, and reproductive health. The Ford Foundation's focus on women is not limited to grants to women and women's organizations; the policy is to have grants targeted at women and to mainstream WID issues in all grants.

Up to 1986, only one person, a WID officer, was formally assigned and paid to integrate gender issues into UNDP programs and projects. In addition, four staff members were designated as WID promoters in each regional bureau, but they were not paid. In 1986, a Division for Women in Development was set up in the UNDP New York headquarters that includes a director and two professional staff members; the UNDP administrator has instructed field offices to assign a staff member to be responsible for considering WID policy at all stages of the UNDP's activities.

Between 1977 and 1987, an adviser on women in development was on the staff of the World Bank, assisted by two to three support staff. Since 1987, as part of the restructuring of the Bank, the position of adviser has been elevated to the status of division chief, with six professional staff members to assist her. WID specialists are beginning to be added to regional offices.

In the Ford Foundation, a circuit-riding program officer, funded in 1976 under the Delegated Authority Project in the International Division of the Foundation in New York, began to provide assistance to field offices in instituting women's programming. When women staff members were hired, part of their responsibilities was to explore potential programs related to women. In 1980, a full-time officer in charge of Foundation-wide women's programs was funded. To oversee the expanding grant program, the Foundation also created the WPG, which reported regularly to the president and the Board of Trustees. In many field offices, the Foundation added new staff members who focused on WID issues or assigned a staff member to be responsible for them. Management instructed all program officers to include WID concerns in their particular program areas. The Foundation's policy was to avoid setting up an administrative WID unit and instead to mainstream the issue by holding all program officers responsible for its consideration.

Explanations of the Different Responses

The characteristics of organizations within the development assistance regime dictate how they respond to WID issues. Table 5.1 describes the relevant features of the three institutions examined in this book.

The Ford Foundation, as a private, voluntary organization, has relatively more opportunity to introduce new issues within the development assistance regime. Because its self-perception is that of a conduit linking governments, disadvantaged groups within countries, NGOs, and other donors, it has been well placed to work on behalf of women. The Foundation, with its normative goal of "finding innovative solutions to social problems"—rather than, for example, the goal of increasing profitability or coordinating technical assistance—is more likely to be responsive to issues that attempt to redefine and broaden the ends to which it is dedicated. The Foundation's goal rests on a value system that emphasizes equity and antidiscrimination. The root of social problems is seen as the unequal treatment of some groups in society. These structural characteristics, of course, do not automatically translate into interest in women's issues. Certain staff members have chosen to act as WID policy entrepreneurs, to build internal consensus that women's issues are important to the Foundation's work. This group has demonstrated through consensus-building activities how the enhancement of women's ability to contribute to and benefit from development on an equal basis with men overcomes discrimination and promotes equity. They success-

Table 5.1 Characteristics of Three Development Assistance Regime Organizations

	UNDP	World Bank	Ford Foundation
Degree of independence within the development assistance regime	Low	Medium	High
Goals	To coordinate technical assistance	To increase profitability; to increase economic growth of borrower nations	To find innovative solutions to social problems
Core values	Self-reliance and sovereignty of member states	Efficiency; promotion of free-market economies	Equality; overcoming discrimination
Procedures	Decentralized decisionmaking with emphasis on administering development activities	Centralized decisionmaking with emphasis on conventional economic analysis	Centralized and decentralized decisionmaking with emphasis on social science analysis
Level of response to to WID issues	Low	Medium	High

fully used political clout as well. WID advocates, instrumental in putting into place new procedures, were aided in their strategies by a supportive president who made WID policy one of his priorities.

Procedures emphasize the search for and solution to social problems. In fact, staff members are primarily social scientists with backgrounds in academia and research organizations. It is also important to note that 53.2 percent of the Foundation's professional staff in 1986 was female.[11] Having more women staff members does not necessarily mean more attention to WID issues, but it does indicate a nondiscriminatory attitude, and it is helpful to have female representatives who deal with WID issues in developing countries, especially in those with traditionally male-dominated societies.

The Foundation's emphasis on finding solutions to social problems has meant support for the production of new knowledge. When the Foundation enters a new area, it makes grants for basic research, applied research, and action programs, in that order. This has proved to be an advantage in women's programming because research by and on women clearly helped to identify program areas in which action needed to be taken. The decisionmaking procedures emphasize easy access to management and encourage local decisionmaking by field representatives. Furthermore, the Foundation makes grants to private voluntary organizations rather than to governments, thus directly aiding private women's organizations. The combination of centralization and decentralization has meant that if top management supports a new issue, program officers, both in the headquarters in New York and in the field offices, have a great deal of leeway to exercise their creativity.

Although it is considered a leader of the development assistance regime, the World Bank has been unwilling to use its role in the case of WID issues, mostly because of the constraints posed by its goals and procedures. The Bank has become involved when other donors and recipient governments have shown interest, but it has otherwise considered WID issues only to the extent that they promote the Bank's goals and fit its procedures. The Bank's goals are to increase its profitability as a financial institution and to promote economic growth in developing countries (with reliance on the market mechanism). When WID issues were presented and justified as being instrumental to these goals, they have been acceptable. Ultimately, the consideration of WID issues depends on the ability of its advocates to demonstrate greater benefit-to-cost ratios in order to command more resources. Generally, women's issues have been linked to a decline in birth rates, which in turn has been linked to increased economic development.

Bank staff members are most comfortable with questions of efficiency and are willing to consider women if their inclusion contributes to more efficient projects. Many staff members pointed out that if it were economically viable, the Bank would consider women, but not *because* they were women. However, the staff is much less comfortable with questions of equity and is generally reluctant to consider women as part of fairness-related issues; there is no good theory to explain the link between equity and economic productivity. Thus, for many economists (who predominate in the Bank's staff), efficiency and productivity are seen as value-neutral and objective, equity as value-laden and subjective.

The Bank's procedures focus on the calculation of economic or financial rates of return. The kinds of analyses required have to be technically rigorous and expressed in quantitative measures of inputs delivered and returns on investment. On the other hand, social analysis, within which WID concerns have generally been placed, is less well accepted and integrated into the Bank's staff work because it is less determinate and requires some experimentation—features that resist traditional cost-benefit analysis. This point is also made by Ascher, who demonstrates how the conventional economic analysis used by the World Bank staff has discouraged the consideration of problems in the environment, human rights, or women in development because such issues are difficult to quantify and require modes of analysis less rigorous than the traditional economic framework.[12] The emphasis on the timely delivery of projects and the pressure on staff members to get a certain number of projects approved in a given amount of time also both act as disincentives for the consideration of women in development. Under this pressure, staff members tend to avoid complex issues that require extra time and experimentation with pilot projects. Consideration of WID concerns would slow down the project approval process and increase complexity of and uncertainty in the staff's work.

WID strategies that take account of the Bank's goals and procedures have been more successful than those that do not. Compared with the previous WID adviser, who followed externally oriented strategies that improved the Bank's image in the development community and emphasized issues of equity and fairness for women, the new WID chief has focused on building alliances with top management, sitting in on high-level management meetings and packaging the WID message as cost-effective. The new WID chief is a population economist, and because the Bank is interested in women in development primarily as a population issue, her credentials give her credibility. She has proposed to focus on making women part of a country's development strategy, incorporating activities into that strategy that would influence the Bank's future advice and lending. She has also suggested theme initiatives: safe motherhood, women in agriculture, and women and work (fact-finding and policy analysis on labor force participation). Furthermore, she has selected major Bank projects or sector loans in agriculture, education, population, health, and nutrition, particularly in Asia and Africa, for a "best effort" to help women.[13] The new WID chief also has been participating in project identification missions, thereby providing WID input at the identification and preparation stages.

The UNDP's response to WID is the most limited among the three agencies—a paradox given that the international women's movement had the greatest opportunity to influence the UN system. The UN system is very decentralized and thus easy to prod, but its decentralization also works to make it harder to move. The UNDP's partners—UN specialized agencies and member governments—have a considerable voice within this tripartite system, and the UNDP is required to give first consideration in project execution to UN executing agencies with the appropriate specialization. Donor governments exercise power in UNDP affairs as contributors of funds, and recipient governments have come to regard the indicative planning figures as firm commitments to their countries. In this system, the UNDP thus needs the approval of its partners on any new policy, including women in development. If recipient governments and UN executing agencies are not interested in WID issues, then the UNDP's response is correspondingly limited.

The decentralized nature of the tripartite system has generally produced a lack of definition of responsibilities (with commensurate authority) with respect to project management. In the case of women in development, this has led to a "passing the buck" syndrome—a disclaiming of responsibility. A good example of this syndrome is the establishment of UNIFEM and the perception within the UNDP that it therefore is not responsible for incorporating WID into its own activities. The decentralized system has not entirely been unfavorable, however. It has allowed gender-sensitive UNDP staff in the field offices to play the role of instigator by bringing donors and recipient governments together to sponsor particular activities.

The overall result of decentralization is the tendency to practice local decisionmaking whereby outcomes depend on the particular interaction among the UNDP resrep, the recipient government, and executing agencies. The implications for WID policy are that women's issues have been considered on an ad hoc basis and generally shaped by the external pressure of gender-sensitive governments and the personal interest of individual UNDP staff members. For example, many UNDP projects with WID components have been instigated and cofunded by the Canadian, Swedish, Norwegian, and Dutch bilateral aid agencies.

The value system that underlies the UNDP's goal is also not particularly favorable for WID policy because it discourages a substantive focus. The UNDP coordinates technical assistance according to member governments' priorities. Its value system emphasizes the self-reliance and self-determination of recipient governments and avoids imposing any external definitions of development. This has meant that the UNDP has lacked a substantive focus and has reflected the interests of its partners and the many mandates assigned to it by the General Assembly.

Because the UNDP is a central administrative agency, the staff and procedures have reflected the emphasis on administrative rules and regulations rather than, for example, technical or substantive skills. Thus, staff members are managers, not focused on learning and experimenting with new substantive areas such as women in development. Given the constraints posed by these goals and procedures, the choices available to WID advocates are limited. First, interest in women in development among staff members is minimal compared with that found in the other two agencies. This lack of interest probably reflects the fact that few information-disseminating activities on WID issues are available for staff members; information is produced by the UNDP Division of Information for external consumption. Bargaining strategies to acquire clout have tended to be externally oriented, focusing on building alliances with the UNDP's partners. Indeed, the strategies of WID advocates increasingly include soliciting support from the UNDP's gender-sensitive partners. For example, the WID advocates in the UNDP have helped to set up a high-level WID training seminar for the executives of UN agencies, including the UNDP administrator, with the cooperation of such gender-sensitive UN agencies as the UNFPA and with funding from Swedish, Norwegian, and Dutch bilateral aid agencies.

Implications of the Findings
for the Empowerment of Women

Overall, the response to WID concerns in the three agencies has increased over time, a reaction prompted by the growing influence of the international women's movement and by increased interest on the part of some donors who were also willing to take a leadership role on behalf of women in development. But the response of aid agencies, as a rule, has been ad hoc; when gender-sensitive actors have come together as cofunders in particular programs and projects, the consideration of WID issues has been more likely, but a systematic incorporation of women's concerns into development activities is only beginning.

The three case studies illustrate not only the importance of organizational goals and procedures in determining policy outcomes but also how social movements must accommodate themselves to these goals and procedures and use them to their advantage if they seek to effect any change within an organization. Penetrating development agencies, however, carries the price of giving up the goal of fundamental changes in favor of reformist ones.

Does this mean we should dismiss work in such development agencies as counterproductive, or the gains made within them on behalf of women in development as insignificant or simply nonexistent? On the contrary, what development agencies can and cannot do for women should be put in context. The case studies demonstrate the success of appropriate bargaining strategies that take account of particular organizational goals and procedures and accommodate them. The response of agencies, likewise, can be evaluated in terms of the extent to which they have empowered women. The stages of empowerment can be ranked from low to high, as shown in Figure 5.1.

Figure 5.1 A Scale of Empowerment

			Criteria
	High	↑	Control
Degree of			Participation
Empowerment			Conscientization
			Access
	Low	↓	Welfare

Source: Karin Himmelstrand, "Can an Aid Bureaucracy Empower Women? The Case of SIDA," *Issue: A Journal of Opinion* 37, 2 (1989): 41.

Within these hierarchically ranked criteria of empowerment, development agencies generally do not invest their energies beyond providing women with welfare and access. As women gain consciousness of their position and potential and increase control of their productive and reproductive lives, this evolution implies changes in social, political, and economic structures that most development agencies are unwilling or unable to address. This reluctance can be attributed to the need to present problems in contractual rather than distributive terms in the quest to alter regimes, but the empowerment of women inevitably implies redistributive arrangements.

Within this general context, what needs to be better understood is how development agencies may constrain or encourage WID policy. Of the three agencies, the UNDP's goals and procedures have constrained it most; the lack of a substantive focus and the difficulty in taking initiatives tend to make the UNDP a follower rather than a leader. On the other hand, its extensive field offices and cooperative development activities provide an opportunity for gender-sensitive field representatives to respond appropriately to local conditions and for the UNDP's gender-sensitive partners to elicit its cooperation in WID projects.

The World Bank's goals and procedures allow the consideration of WID concerns as a means to increased economic productivity. The Bank is unwilling directly to tackle such issues as women's participation and control over their lives. On the other hand, it is in a position to channel resources to women by means of policy advice to borrower governments. For example, one issue the Bank may discuss with borrower governments in the future is how they can facilitate the activities of NGOs (including women's organizations) for the purpose of development.

The Ford Foundation has, on the whole, initiated and encouraged WID policy in the development community. Its activities have gone beyond providing women with welfare and access to facilitating research on and by women and to helping form women's organizations whose goal is to enable women to take control of their lives. The reason for this favorable response to women in development is that the Foundation's goals permit it to deal directly with overcoming discrimination against women. It especially sees itself in a position to voice the concerns and interests of groups hitherto excluded from the benefits of society. Focusing on innovative approaches to development and experimentation, the Foundation is an especially well-placed ally of the international women's movement. As one staff member stated: "The Foundation offices function as a conduit, as a catalyst to build links between governments, nongovernmental organizations, and other donor agencies."

How regimes are altered and how the altered norms and rules get translated into action within specific organizational contexts may be examined in both theoretical and practical terms. In theoretical terms, inquiry expands our understanding of regime change and of organizational response to new issues when new constituencies enter into the political arena, and this holds important implications for our analysis of all regimes and international movements that attempt to bring about changes at the international as well as organizational levels. In practical terms, our inquiry highlights the necessity of informed policy advocacy in order to bring about change.

What I suggest in this book is that social movements have an opportunity to affect existing norms in decentralized, weak regimes, but when those norms have to be translated into policy, organizational characteristics determine the nature of the response. The three case studies demonstrate that structural factors, the particular position of an organization in a regime, and the fit of a new issue into organizational goals and procedures all shape response. Without the conscious choice of some staff members to act as advocates of the new issue, the response may never be formulated.

Notes

1. Ashworth, "The United Nations Women's Conference and International Linkages with the Women's Movement"; Tinker, *Women in Washington*.

2. The following discussion draws from Charlotte Bunch, "The Growth of Women's Movements in the United States and the Third World: Challenges of the Next Decade," in Ford Foundation, "The Changing Context for Movements to Improve Women's Lives," 29 September 1986.

3. Mayra Buvinic, "Trends in Donor Approaches to Women and Income in the Third World: A Discussion Paper for the Ford Foundation," presented at the Symposium on Expanding Income-Earning Opportunities for Women in Poverty: A Cross-Regional Dialogue, Nairobi, May 1–5, 1988.

4. Young, "Politics of International Regime Formation."

5. Schattschneider, *Semi-Sovereign People*.

6. Young, "Politics of International Regime Formation," p. 371.

7. Anne Costain and Douglas Costain, "The Women's Lobby: Impact of a Movement on Congress," in *Interest Group Politics*, eds. Allan Cigler and Loomis Burdett (Washington, DC: Congressional Quarterly Inc., 1983).

8. World Bank, *Operations Manual*, OMS 2.20, section f, Sociological Aspects.

9. The general reserve serves as a flexible instrument for meeting unanticipated needs and responding to unusual program opportunities in the Ford Foundation.

10. Data provided by the Ford Foundation, covering up to and including March 1988.

11. Ford Foundation, *Created Equal*. Women number approximately 20 percent of staff at the World Bank and the UNDP.

12. Ascher, "New Development Approaches."

13. World Bank, "Proposed Work Program for Women in Development."

Bibliography

Acharya, Meena, and Lynn Bennett. *Women in the Subsistence Sector: Economic Participation and Household Decision-Making in Nepal.* Staff Working Paper 526. Washington, DC: World Bank, 1983.

Ascher, William. "New Development Approaches and the Adaptability of International Agencies: The Case of the World Bank." *International Organization* 37, 3 (Summer 1983): 415–439.

Ashworth, Georgina. "The United Nations Women's Conference and International Linkages with the Women's Movement." In *Pressure Groups in the Global System*, ed. E. Willetts. London: Francis Pinter, 1982.

Ayres, Robert. *Banking on the Poor.* Cambridge: Massachusetts Institute of Technology Press, 1984.

Bardach, Eugene. *The Implementation Game.* Cambridge: Massachusetts Institute of Technology Press, 1978.

Baum, Warren, and Stokes M. Tolbert. *Investing in Development: Lessons of World Bank Experience.* Washington, DC: World Bank, 1985.

Boserup, Ester. *Women's Role in Economic Development.* New York: St. Martin's Press, 1970.

Boulding, Elise. *Women: The Fifth World.* New York: Foreign Policy Association, 1980.

Bratton, Michael. "The Comrades and the Countryside: The Politics of Agricultural Policy in Zimbabwe." *World Politics* 39, 2 (January 1987): 174–202.

Briscoe, John, and David de Ferranti. *Water for Rural Communities: Helping People to Help Themselves.* Washington, DC: World Bank, 1987.

Buvinic, Mayra. "Trends in Donor Approaches to Women and Income in the Third World: A Discussion Paper for the Ford Foundation." Paper presented at the Symposium on Expanding Income-Earning Opportunities for Women in Poverty: A Cross-Regional Dialogue, Nairobi, May 1–5, 1988.

Buvinic, Mayra, et al. *Women's Issues in Third World Poverty.* Baltimore, MD: John Hopkins Press, 1983.

Costain, Anne, and Douglas Costain. "The Women's Lobby: Impact of a Movement on Congress." In *Interest Group Politics*, eds. Allan Cigler and Loomis Burdett. Washington, DC: Congressional Quarterly Inc., 1983.

Cox, Robert. "The Executive Head: An Essay in Leadership in International

Organization." In *International Organization: Politics and Process*, eds. Leland Goodrich and David Kay. Madison: University of Wisconsin Press, 1973.

Cox, Robert, and Harold Jacobson. *The Anatomy of Influence.* New Haven, CT: Yale University Press, 1974.

Demongeot, Patrick. "U.N. System Development Assistance." In *U.S. Foreign Assistance: Investment or Folly?* eds. John Wilhelm and Gerry Feinstein. New York: Praeger, 1984.

Derthick, Martha. *New Towns in Town.* Washington, DC: Urban Institute, 1972.

Downs, Anthony. *Inside Bureaucracy.* Boston: Little, Brown, 1966.

Flora, Cornelia Butler. "Incorporating Women into International Development Programs: The Political Phenomenology of a Private Foundation." *Women & Politics* 2, 4 (Winter 1982): 89–106.

Food and Agricultural Organization of the United Nations. The Women in Agricultural Production and Rural Development Service. "Training in WID/Gender Analysis in Agricultural Development: A Review of Experiences and Lessons." Unpublished paper, July 1989.

Ford Foundation. *That 51 %.* New York: Ford Foundation, April 1974.

Ford Foundation. *That 51 % Plus.* New York: Ford Foundation, February 1979.

Ford Foundation. "Programs for Women: An Information Paper for the Board of Trustees." Unpublished paper, December 1979.

Ford Foundation. *Women in the World.* New York: Ford Foundation, 1980.

Ford Foundation. "Programs for Women: Plans and Budgets for Fiscal Years 1980 and 1981." Unpublished paper, March 1980.

Ford Foundation. "Interim Report on the Expanded Women's Program." Unpublished paper, February 1981.

Ford Foundation. "Women's Programs: Past, Present and Future." Unpublished paper, June 1986.

Ford Foundation. "The Changing Context for Movements to Improve Women's Lives: Proceedings of the Ford Foundation's Women's Program Forum." Unpublished paper, 29 September 1986.

Ford Foundation. *Created Equal.* New York: Ford Foundation, October 1986.

Ford Foundation. *1987 Annual Report.* New York: Ford Foundation, 1987.

Ford Foundation. *Current Interests 1988 and 1989.* New York: Ford Foundation, 1988.

Freeman, Jo. *The Politics of Women's Liberation.* New York: Longman, 1975.

Germain, Adrienne. "Poor Rural Women: A Policy Perspective." *Journal of International Affairs* 30, 2 (1976–77): 161–172.

Herz, Barbara, and Anthony R. Measham. *Safe Motherhood Initiative: Proposals for Action.* Discussion Paper No. 9. Washington, DC: World Bank, 1987.

Himmelstrand, Karin. "Can an Aid Bureaucracy Empower Women? The Case of SIDA." *Issue: A Journal of Opinion* 37, 2 (1989): 37–43.

Jaquette, Jane. "Women and Modernization Theory: A Decade of Feminist Criticism." *World Politics* 34, 2 (1982): 267–284.

Karaosmanoglu, Atilla. "The U.N. Decade for Women." *The Bank's World* (September 1985): 12–13.

Kay, David A., and Harold K. Jacobson. *Environmental Protection: The International Dimension.* Totowa, NJ: Allanheld & Osmun, 1983.

Knott, Jack. "The Multiple and Ambiguous Roles of Professionals in Public Policymaking." *Knowledge Creation, Diffusion, Utilization* 8, 1 (1986): 131–153.

Korten, David. "Third-Generation NGO Strategies: A Key to People-Centered Development." *World Development* 15 (Autumn 1987).

Krasner, Stephen D., ed. *International Regimes.* Ithaca, NY: Cornell University Press, 1983.

Kudat, Ayse. *Communications, Women and Settlements Management.* Working Paper. Washington, DC: EDI/World Bank, 1988.

Kudat, Ayse. *Women's Participation in Human Settlements Management.* Working Paper. Washington, DC: EDI/World Bank, 1988.

Kudat, Ayse. *Women's Participation in Rural Road Maintenance in Sub-Saharan Africa.* Working Paper. Washington, DC: EDI/World Bank, 1988.

Kudat, Ayse, and Helen Abadzi. *Women's Presence in Arab Higher Education: Linking School, Labor Markets and Social Roles.* Working Paper. Washington, DC: EDI/World Bank, 1989.

Leeds, Ruth. "The Absorption of Protest: A Working Paper." In *New Perspectives in Organizational Research,* eds. W. W. Cooper, H. J. Leavitt, and M. W. Shelly II. New York: Wiley, 1964.

Lethem, Francis, and Heli Perrett. *Human Factors in Project Work.* Staff Working Paper 397. Washington, DC: World Bank, June 1980.

Levy, Frank, Arthur Meltsner, and Aaron Wildavsky. *Urban Outcomes.* Berkeley: University of California Press, 1974.

Lewis, Barbara. *Invisible Farmers: Women and the Crisis in Agriculture.* Washington, DC: USAID, 1981.

Maguire, Patricia. *Women in Development: An Alternative Analysis.* Amherst: Center for International Education, University of Massachusetts, 1984.

McWilliams, Nancy. "Contemporary Feminism, Consciousness-Raising, and Changing Views of the Political." In *Women and Politics,* ed. Jane Jaquette. New York: Wiley, 1974.

Mohan, Rakesh. *Labor Force Participation in a Developing Metropolis: Does Sex Matter?* Staff Working Paper 749. Washington, DC: World Bank, 1985.

Molnar, Augusta, and Gotz Schreiber. *Women and Forestry: Operational Issues.* Policy, Planning and Research Working Paper, WPS 184. Washington, DC: World Bank, May 1989.

Ness, Gayle, and Steven Brechin. "Bridging the Gap: International Organizations as Organizations." *International Organization* 42, 2 (Spring 1988): 245–273.

Polsby, Nelson. *Policy Innovation in the United States.* New Haven, CT: Yale University Press, 1984.

Pressman, Jeffrey, and Aaron Wildavsky. *Implementation.* Berkeley: University of California Press, 1973.

Rogers, Barbara. *The Domestication of Women: Discrimination in Developing Societies.* New York: St. Martin's Press, 1979; and London: Tavistock, 1980.

Schattschneider, E. E. *The Semi-Sovereign People.* New York: Holt, Rinehart & Winston, 1960.

Scott, Gloria, and Marilyn Carr. *The Impact of Technology Choice on Rural Women in Bangladesh: Problems and Opportunities.* Staff Working Paper 731. Washington, DC: World Bank, 1985.

Scott, Richard. *Organizations: Rational, Natural and Open Systems.* Englewood Cliffs, NJ: Prentice-Hall, 1987.

Shields, Nwanganga. *Women in the Urban Labor Markets in Africa: The Case of Tanzania.* Staff Working Paper 380, Washington, DC: World Bank, 1980.

Starrs, Ann. *Preventing the Tragedy of Maternal Deaths—Report on the International Safe Motherhood Conference, Nairobi, Kenya, February 1987.* Washington, DC: World Bank, 1987.

Staudt, Kathleen. "Bureaucratic Resistance to Women's Programs: The Case of Women in Development." In *Women, Power and Policy,* ed. Ellen Bonaparth. New York: Pergamon Press, 1982.

Staudt, Kathleen. *Women, Foreign Assistance and Advocacy Administration.* New York: Praeger, 1983.

Staudt, Kathleen. "Women's Politics and Capitalist Transformation in Sub-Saharan Africa." Women in Development Working Paper Series No. 54. East Lansing, MI: Michigan State University, 1984.

Tendler, Judith. *Inside Foreign Aid.* Baltimore, MD: Johns Hopkins University Press, 1975.

Tinker, Irene, ed. *Women in Washington: Advocates for Public Policy.* New York: Pergamon Press; London: Sage, 1983.

Tinker, Irene, and M. B. Bramsen, eds. *Women and World Development.* Washington, DC: Overseas Development Council, 1976.

United Nations. *Newsletter on the Status of Women* (June 1974).

United Nations. International Women's Year Secretariat. *Meeting in Mexico: World Conference of the International Women's Year 1975.* New York: Center for Economic and Social Information, 1975.

United Nations. General Assembly. "United Nations Decade for Women: Equality, Development and Peace: Financial and Technical Support Activities of Relevant Organizations and Bodies of the United Nations System." (A/36/485), 16 September 1981.

United Nations. *Nairobi Forward-Looking Strategies for the Advancement of Women.* New York: UN Division for Economic and Social Information, April 1986.

United Nations. "Aid Where It Works." *Development Forum* 15, 2 (March 1987): 1, 4.

United Nations. "World Bank Poverty Pledge." *Development Forum.* 15, 1 (January-February 1987): 1, 12.

United Nations. *Equal Time* (double midyear issue, 1987).

United Nations Development Programme. "Female Imperatives in Development." *UNDP News* (January-February 1975): 15–16.

United Nations Development Programme. "Guidelines on the Integration of Women in Development." G3100-1, 25 February 1977.

United Nations Development Programme. "Integration of Women in Development—Implementation of Governing Council Decision 80/22/II." (UNDP/PROG/79; UNDP/PROG/FIELD/120), 12 February 1981.

United Nations Development Programme. "Report of the Mission to Evaluate the UNDP/ECA Programs for the Integration of Women in Development, 7 May–7 July 1984." Unpublished paper.

United Nations Development Programme. *Generation: Portrait of the United*

Nations Development Programme: 1950–1985. New York: Division of Information, 1985.

United Nations Development Programme. *Women's Participation in Development: An Inter-Organizational Assessment.* Evaluation Study 13. New York: UNDP, June 1985.

United Nations Development Programme. *Is There a Better Way?* New York: Division of Information, June 1985.

United Nations Development Programme. *A Better Environment for Development—1986 Annual Report.* New York: UNDP, 1986.

United Nations Development Programme. "Programme Implementation—Women in Development: Implementation Strategy." (DP/1986/14), 26 February 1986.

United Nations Development Programme. Bureau for Programme and Policy Evaluation. Technical Advisory Division. "Draft UNDP Programme Advisory Note: Women in Development." Unpublished paper, May 1986.

United Nations Development Programme. Governing Council. "Statement by Denmark on behalf of the Nordic Countries." 33d Sess., 12 June 1986.

United Nations Development Programme. Governing Council. "Response by William H. Draper III." 33d Sess. 12 June 1986.

United Nations Development Programme. "Programme Implementation—The Implementation of Decisions Adopted by the Governing Council at Previous Sessions: Women in Development." (DP/1987/15), 20 April 1987.

United Nations Development Programme. Division of Women in Development. "Women in Development: Policy and Procedures." Unpublished paper, 17 November 1987.

United Nations Development Programme. Governing Council. "Programme Implementation—UNDP Cooperation with Non-Governmental Organizations and Grass-Roots Organizations; Women in Development—Report of the Administrator." (DP/1988/15/Add.1), 11 May 1988.

United Nations Development Programme. *Women in Development—Project Achievement Reports from the UNDP.* New York: UNDP, June 1988.

United Nations Development Programme. *Women in Development News—WIDLINK* (September 1988).

United Nations Development Programme. Governing Council. "Programme Implementation—UNDP Cooperation with Non-Governmental Organizations and Grass-Roots Organizations; Women in Development; Report of the Administrator." (DP/1988/15), 10 March 1988.

United Nations Development Programme. Governing Council. "Programme Implementation—Implementation of Decisions Adopted by the Governing Council at Previous Sessions: Women in Development." (DP/1989/24), 15 March 1989.

United Nations Development Programme. Division for Women in Development. "An Amalgamation of WID Reviews of Eleven Countries' Country Programmes." Unpublished paper, June 1989.

United Nations Development Programme. *Women in Development—Project Achievement Reports from the UNDP.* New York: UNDP, June 1989.

United Nations Development Programme. "Girl Guides Inspire Health in Thailand's Poor Northeast." *Source* (December 1989): 15–17.

U.S. Congress. House of Representatives. *Foreign Assistance Act.* 93d Cong. 2d sess., PL 93-189, Sections 103-107, 17 December 1973.

U.S. Department of State, Agency for International Development, "Integration of Women into National Economies." Policy Determination 60, 16 September 1974.

Wellesley Editorial Committee, ed. *Women and National Development: The Complexities of Change.* Chicago: University of Chicago Press, 1977.

Wheeler, David. "Female Education, Family Planning, Income, and Population: A Long-run Econometric Simulation Model." In *Three Cross-Country Analyses of the Effects of Organized Family Planning,* ed. Nancy Birdsall. Washington, DC: World Bank, 1984.

Wildavsky, Aaron. "The Self-Evaluating Organization." *Public Administration Review* (September-October 1972): 509–519.

Wilson, James Q. "Innovation in Organization: Notes Toward a Theory." In *Approaches to Organizational Design,* ed. J. D. Thompson. Pittsburgh, PA: University of Pittsburgh Press, 1966.

World Bank. *Questions and Answers: The World Bank and IDA.* Washington, DC: World Bank, January 1974.

World Bank. *Rural Development.* Sector Policy Paper. Washington, DC: World Bank, February 1975.

World Bank. *Abstract of Current Studies: The World Bank Research Program.* Washington, DC: World Bank, 1978.

World Bank. Office of the Adviser on Women in Development. "Forestry Projects and Women." Unpublished paper, September 1980.

World Bank. Office of the Adviser on Women in Development. "A Framework for Analysis." Unpublished paper prepared for the Workshop for Women in Development, 19–21 January 1983.

World Bank. *Abstract of Current Studies: The World Bank Research Program.* Washington, DC: World Bank, 1984.

World Bank. *The World Bank Annual Report 1984.* Washington, DC: World Bank, 1984.

World Bank. *World Development Report 1984.* London: Oxford University Press, 1984.

World Bank. *Tenth Annual Review of Project Performance Audit Results.* Washington, DC: World Bank, 1985.

World Bank. *The World Bank Annual Report 1985.* Washington, DC: World Bank, 1985.

World Bank. *Agricultural Research and Extension: Evaluation of the World Bank's Experience.* Washington, DC: World Bank, 1985.

World Bank. Technology Advisory Group. *Involving Women in Sanitation Project Planning and Implementation.* Washington, DC: World Bank, 1985.

World Bank. "Indonesian Women and Development." Unpublished paper, April 30, 1985.

World Bank. "Q and A with Gloria Scott." *The Bank's World,* 4, 9 (September 1985): 4–8.

World Bank. "The U.N. Decade for Women." *The Bank's World,* 4, 9 (September 1985): 11–12.

World Bank. *1985 Annual Review of Project Performance Results.* Washington, DC: World Bank, 1986.

World Bank. Operations Evaluation Department. *Cotton Development Programs in Burkina Faso, Cote d'Ivoire, and Togo.* Washington, DC: World Bank, 1988.

World Bank. *The World Bank Annual Report 1989.* Washington, DC: World Bank, 1989.

Young, Oran. "The Politics of International Regime Formation: Managing Natural Resources and the Environment." *International Organization* 43, 3 (Summer 1989): 349–375.

Index

About the Book and the Author

Despite more than a decade of emphasis on the plight of Third World women, the incorporation of women fully into development activities has been a slow and uneven process. Nüket Kardam explores three of the most influential international development agencies—the United Nations Development Programme, the World Bank, and the Ford Foundation—to determine why this is the case.

Kardam has interviewed key personnel and examined internal documents in the three agencies, as well as drawn extensively on previous studies. Identifying the key variables affecting the ways and extent to which women have been brought into development policy formulation, she finds that the decentralization of the UNDP inhibits women's issues from coming to the fore, while the World Bank's emphasis on economic analysis, to the exclusion of social concerns, limits its ability to respond to women's needs and potential contributions. In contrast, the Ford Foundation's proclivity toward fostering egalitarianism encourages the consideration of women in its programs.

Kardam's study has major implications for the process of formulating effective development policies in general, as well as for issues related specifically to women in development.

Nüket Kardam is assistant professor in the Department of Government, Pomona College.